What
Matters
Most

What Matters Most

LESSONS THE DYING
TEACH US ABOUT LIVING

Diane Button

THE OPEN FIELD · PENGUIN LIFE

VIKING

An imprint of Penguin Random House LLC
1745 Broadway, New York, NY 10019
penguinrandomhouse.com

The Open Field/A Penguin Life Book

Designed by Alexis Sulaimani

ISBN 9780593833889 (hardcover)
ISBN 9780593833896 (ebook)

Printed in the United States of America
1st Printing

The authorized representative in the EU for
product safety and compliance is Penguin Random House
Ireland, Morrison Chambers, 32 Nassau Street, Dublin
D02 YH68, Ireland, https://eu-contact.penguin.ie.

MARIA SHRIVER
PRESENTS
THE OPEN FIELD
A PUBLISHING IMPRINT
BOOKS THAT RISE ABOVE THE NOISE AND MOVE HUMANITY FORWARD

Dear Reader,

Years ago, these words attributed to Rumi found a place in my heart:

> *Out beyond ideas of*
> *wrongdoing and rightdoing,*
> *there is a field. I'll meet you there.*

Ever since, I've cultivated an image of what I call "the Open Field"—a place out beyond fear and shame, beyond judgment, loneliness, and expectation. A place that hosts the reunion of all creation. It's the hope of my soul to find my way there—and whenever I hear an insight or a practice that helps me on the path, I love nothing more than to share it with others.

That's why I've created The Open Field. My hope is to publish books that honor the most unifying truth in human life: We are all seeking the same things. We're all seeking dignity. We're all seeking joy. We're all seeking love and acceptance, seeking to be seen, to be safe. And there is no competition for these things we seek—because they are not material goods; they are spiritual gifts!

We can all give each other these gifts if we share what we know—what has lifted us up and moved us forward. That is our duty to one another—to help each other toward acceptance, toward peace, toward happiness—and my promise to you is that the books published under this imprint will be maps to the Open Field, written by guides who know the path and want to share it.

Each title will offer insights, inspiration, and guidance for moving beyond the fears, the judgments, and the masks we all wear. And when we take off the masks, guess what? We will see that we are the opposite of what we thought—we are each other.

We are all on our way to the Open Field. We are all helping one another along the path. I'll meet you there.

Love, Maria S

To my Grandpa Charlie,
who loved me quietly but fiercely.

To my clients, who trusted me
with their tender stories and final moments.

While we wait here and wonder . . .
they already know.

CONTENTS

AUTHOR'S NOTE

This book is a work of nonfiction, written for the purpose of sharing stories, experiences, wisdom, and personal perspectives about living from people facing death. Each client profiled in this book was someone we supported, held, and deeply cared for. Due to the sensitive material, some names and identifying details have been changed to protect privacy. In other cases, permission has been granted to use their personal names and details.

Throughout this book, we address topics including death, dying, loss, and grief. Please be aware that this is sensitive and potentially emotionally triggering material. If you are grieving a recent loss, tending to your own heart might include avoiding reading other grief stories until you are ready.

The stories you are about to read have changed me profoundly, from the inside out. My greatest hope is that these courageous people and their personal journeys will also inspire you to embrace what truly matters, let go of what doesn't, and guide you to enjoy and cherish the gift of every precious day.

INTRODUCTION

I'm a death doula, a companion for the dying. The sad part about my work is that all my clients die. The beautiful part is they all leave so much of themselves behind for us to learn and grow from.

I was introduced to death at an early age. Through a school community service project, I began volunteering and then continued working at the Nazareth House, a convalescent home just a short walk across the street from my high school. I knew the names, dietary needs, birthdays, and special food requests of all the residents. As they became bedridden, I took the trays to their rooms and fed them whenever I had the time. It wasn't part of my job description, but I loved to sit with them and listen to their stories.

I was a kid, just fifteen years old, with my life ahead of me. The residents I cared for were on the other end of the life cycle. They wanted to share their stories of love and loss, and to reminisce about old times with someone who was willing to listen. Often, we perused photo albums filled with a lifetime of memories from generations past. Some residents were satisfied and at peace with the lives they had lived, while others shared heartbreaking stories about dreams that never came true. I learned very early that sometimes just letting someone tell their story can be so healing.

In my next job, I worked in the admissions department at a hospital emergency room, where I witnessed doctors and nurses dealing daily with people on the edge of life and death. I became acutely aware of the precious and uncertain quality of life and how unsuspecting and unprepared we are when it comes to facing our mortality. Unlike the long-term residents of Nazareth House, most of those who did not make it out of the emergency room never had the chance to say goodbye.

By the time I was thirty, I had been with quite a few people at the end of their lives. But when my Grandpa Charlie died in my arms, something happened inside me that still feels like the most spiritually meaningful moment of my life.

My grandfather was my hero. When I was a little girl, I felt like he was 100 percent present, wherever he was. If he was talking to me, then I was the only person who mattered to him at that moment. He made me feel important, valued, and special. I wasn't the only one who idolized him. He was a renowned San Francisco plastic surgeon who specialized in treating severe burn victims. He witnessed excruciating pain and suffering, and he grieved deeply with the families who lost loved ones he could not save. He was humble and kind, and he held himself with a confidence that was devoid of arrogance and full of compassion and the desire to heal the hurting people he served.

At the age of eighty-four, Grandpa Charlie was diagnosed with lung cancer. In a matter of months, it metastasized throughout his body and into his brain, causing him to need full-time care. It was an honor to cook and care for him, but heartbreaking to bear witness to this brilliant, loving man losing his independence more and more each day.

One night, just days before he died, my mom decided to make my grandfather his favorite home-cooked meal of lamb chops with mint jelly, mashed potatoes, green beans, and strawberry shortcake for dessert. The entire family gathered at the same round table where we had eaten countless meals together for over twenty years. My grandfather was so peaceful. He had Frank Sinatra crooning in the background from the antique Victrola, a delicious feast, and his family surrounding him. I watched as he devoured his meal and giggled to myself as he repeatedly spooned a heaping portion of mint jelly over every small bite of the lamb chop.

At one point, he took a giant bite, put his fork down, and looked at each of us very slowly. I felt he was telling me he loved me and saying goodbye. My brother thought he was thinking about all the memories of his life spent with us. Then my grandfather leaned forward. I leaned forward, too, just waiting for the words that I thought were surely going to be emblazoned on my heart and soul forever.

He paused and slowly said, "When I die . . . I'm really going to miss . . . mint jelly."

We all chuckled at my grandfather's comment because it was funny and unexpected, but also because we were not surprised. My grandfather loved us in his own way, fiercely and often silently. He showed me that there are many ways we can express love, and it isn't always with words.

The following week when my grandfather died, he was smiling. The breeze was blowing as the church bells rang, filling the bedroom with an angelic song of peace. I stared in awe at his face, and that gentle, giant smile, realizing immediately that I would never have the chance to ask him what fulfilled him and brought him such calmness and peace. I wanted to know more about my grandfather. I wanted to know what made him die with such a big smile on his face.

That is where this journey began for me.

Exploring a Meaningful Life

After my grandfather died, I read everything I could find about death and dying. I attended seminars, watched movies, and talked to older people in parks, on airplanes, or wherever I met them. Over the years, my understanding about love, relationships, grief, loss, living well, and dying in peace continued growing with every new conversation, but I was still curious about that smile on my grandfather's face.

His gentle smile led me back to college, where I earned a master's degree in counseling psychology just so I could study death and dying. Still, nothing really clicked to explain his giant smile until I began working on my thesis, which explored the components of a meaningful life, a phenomenological study of those age seventy-five and older who felt like their lives had been fulfilling and they could die in peace, knowing they were ready.

What did I learn from this research? I learned that love matters. Relationships matter. Making a difference and being kind matters. Faith and spiritual beliefs matter, too, adding another layer of preparation and comfort to those at the end of life.

I also noticed there are some common threads that tie us all together. Everyone I interviewed described the typical highs and lows, and the good times and not so good times that we all experience over the course of a lifetime. No one can avoid this. The secret lies in how we respond to those peaks and valleys. That's what defines us, separates us, and makes us human. That's what motivates us, inspires us, challenges us, and gives us a reason to get up every day and seek the joy and goodness that come from living a full and meaningful life. When these seniors reached the final stage of their lives, they were not burdened with unfinished business, unhealed relationships, or anything that would keep them from feeling prepared to die, at least from an emotional standpoint. They were ready.

I finally felt I was starting to understand a little more about my grandfather and that smile. He was unburdened. He was emotionally free and spiritually at peace. He lived a meaningful life.

The Doula Path

My journey toward understanding what matters most in this life took some twists and turns, including my own personal journey with breast cancer, some deep experiences with grief and loss, and many years as a hospice volunteer working with people facing death. One day while meeting with a hospice coordinator, I learned about an emerging field of end-of-life workers known as death doulas, and immediately my interest was piqued. Within weeks I was taking classes and soon became a companion for the dying, supporting people in their final weeks, months, or days on earth.

I don't take my job lightly, as often these are the most profound days of someone's life, filled with raw emotion, curiosity, meaning, and truth. People ask me how I can do the emotionally difficult or "sad" work of being a death doula, but I find it to be uplifting, enlightening, and often even joyful.

Many years ago, when I was new to the calling, I vividly remember sitting anxiously in my car with sweaty palms and a racing heart after pulling up to a new client's house for the first time, and sometimes for the second and third time. I knew this was important work, and that it was an honor to be entrusted with this sacred time. But like all of us who support people at the end of life, I have never died before. To this day, I believe there are emotions and thoughts that dying people experience that I will never fully understand until it is my turn.

Still, it would be impossible to fully capture the connection I have with my clients because, in many ways, it is otherworldly. It is beyond the scope of yesterday, today, and tomorrow. It defies time as we know it, yet it is immersed in the present tense, two sets of eyes staring into the unknown . . . together. My clients are leaving the familiarity of this life, while I will be staying here paying bills and sitting in traffic, wondering about their journey as they move on to the great unknown. Yet in those moments, when I'm at the bedside and we lock eyes, we are 100 percent here, together, and present.

My work is a privilege. Every time I am invited to sit at the bedside of a dying person is an incredible honor that I will never take for granted. Their eyes can tell the story of an entire life. I see joy, regret, laughter, and sadness. I see struggles and victories, graduations, weddings, parties, and backyard barbecues. I see the complexity and the simplicity. When someone is dying, and they have called a death doula, it is because they want to get real. They want to fully experience this new phase of their life, the ultimate transition, and they want to do it consciously and with someone who is not afraid to settle into the hard corners of the room with them. And sometimes they are scared. These are the spaces where most people don't feel comfortable venturing if they don't have to, but there is often so much waiting to be discovered.

A death doula shows up prepared, yet without expectations. We bring our hearts to this work first, knowing that the human connection is our most important tool. From there, we have our doula tools, the skills we have honed over time to offer our clients an opportunity to explore their emotions, consider what they may still want to do, and talk through what matters most as they prepare themselves for their end of life.

Over the years, I've created and learned about many tools to support my clients through their dying time. For some, understanding the components of a meaningful life gives them a foundation to contemplate what might be most important. For others, engaging in a life review and discussing what they have experienced over the decades can bring up areas that may need some special care. Many clients express that it feels important that they are not forgotten. For them, organizing a personalized legacy project can bring joy while they are alive, and leave a lasting memory when they are gone. In addition, I've developed a list of simple questions I ask almost all my clients to help guide our time together and give them a moment to reflect on the present moment. These questions and tools will be explored in detail in this book.

Even if you have all the tools and support available, sometimes people suffer at the end of life. But bearing witness to some messy and challenging experiences has been a powerful and motivating teacher, too. Over time I've learned that I don't need to know what to say in advance and I can't possibly know what awaits me when I enter my client's living space. I need to simply be open, step in without an agenda, and let each visit unfold naturally. My clients are in charge. So now when I arrive at a client's house, I pause and hold space for whatever happens that day. I breathe. I pray. I set my personal story aside. And then I knock on the door.

The Wisdom Keepers

This book exists because of an article I wrote for Maria Shriver's *Sunday Paper* about the lessons for living I have learned from the dying. The article went viral, and I still receive emails from people who have read it, all eager to share their stories and express gratitude for my writing an article that inspired them to live differently and to engage in conversations about living well and dying well, too.

Of course, there are endless lessons from the dying, and it was difficult to pick just ten for the *Sunday Paper*, so this book is an opportunity to share even more of their stories. We will explore the ways you can use these lessons to feel a sense of wholeness and to find meaning, joy, and a peace that surpasses all understanding in your everyday life. These invaluable insights come from deep, purposeful, heartfelt, and sometimes hard conversations with my clients, or those I refer to as the "wisdom keepers." They are my greatest teachers. Where else can I learn the secrets of life? Where else can I go to fill my soul with peace and my heart with an understanding of love that knows no boundaries? Where else can I find pure truth, unmasked and vulnerable, afraid but willing?

I can say with great conviction that when someone is facing death, they are aware of things that those of us who speed to yoga class are not always paying attention to. The superficial and unimportant entrapments of life are stripped away, making space for what matters most. Priorities shift, values deepen, and some people change radically. Some of my clients say colors are more vibrant, people are more beautiful, and that they notice the simplicity of creation all around them. I've listened with joy to detailed descriptions of a single yellow flower sprouting in the crack of a sidewalk, or the way the grated Parmesan cheese melts slowly into a bowl of fresh pasta. The world looks different and priorities change when time is short and your future can be measured in days or weeks, rather than years.

In some ways, this surprised me when I first began working with the dying. Perhaps due to my own need for organization and preparation, I imagined that people living with a terminal diagnosis would be busy organizing their finances, cleaning out their underwear drawers, and moving at warp speed to get everything squeezed into whatever time they had left. Some of this planning and preparation is necessary and important, and often exactly what happens when someone is first diagnosed. But as news of a life-limiting illness settles in and people begin to pause and reflect, the urgency often shifts to a more heart-centered way of choosing priorities and focusing on well-being in their everyday life. They want to finish well and spend their days living in alignment with their values and purpose. They want to explore meaning, forgiveness, and love, and to be sure they are taking the time to do and say the things that matter most. There is no time to waste in one's final days.

In this book, I'd like to gently ask you, What about today? Are you wasting too much precious time, or speeding through life without pausing to ask yourself if you are experiencing joy or finding meaning? Are you missing the moments? What if some of the lessons we death doulas have learned from the dying could be available for you to incorporate into your daily life? What if you could live your life in a way that invited you into this contemplative place now?

Why wait until you are dying to understand what makes a meaningful life? Why not start today?

To die with gratitude, you must learn to live with gratitude.

To die with a joyful heart, you must learn to live with a joyful heart.

To die with a clean slate, you must learn to live with a clean slate.

To die surrounded by love, you must live surrounded by love.

To die in harmony with all beings, you must live in harmony with all beings.

To die in peace, you must learn to live in peace.

To die well, you must learn to live well.

What
Matters
Most

My Name Is
Floyd Barker

Have you ever met someone who changed the way you see the world? I've had many epiphanies in my work with the dying, but this book would not exist if not for Floyd. He cracked the door open for me, giving me a glimpse into how to truly be a doula, and how to meet someone where they are . . . quickly, kindly, and without a hint of procedural red tape. He taught me how to hold love and grief at the same time, and to honor all the emotions that make us human. But most of all, Floyd showed me the importance of listening, of connecting, and of caring for each other.

Floyd was lonely. He was also dying from kidney failure, but it was the loneliness and grief that were causing his greatest suffering. You couldn't tell from his gregarious smile and inquisitive eyes, but it was there, deep down and ever present. He was eighty-eight years old and still living alone in the rustic farmhouse he had shared with his late wife, Ruth, for more than sixty years. Reminders of their life together filled the walls and bookcases, and photos covered the tops of the old pine dressers. This was their home, and he didn't want to change anything. Ruth died six years before, and Floyd knew he was stuck and living in the past. He wanted to talk to a death doula about letting go a little to free up some emotional energy to see friends, socialize, and maybe even feel some joy again.

Floyd and Ruth were creatures of habit. They enjoyed a daily breakfast routine, which they had prepared the same way for decades. Every morning, if the sun was shining, they would take their favorite mugs filled with French roast coffee and full cream, along with a warm, buttery croissant, out on the porch, sit quietly side by side in their chairs, and listen to the birds. This was the first ritual they shared every day, but far from the last. They were intertwined in every way, and Floyd continued with their daily routines as the years went by . . . without Ruth.

The chair next to him was Ruth's chair, he told me. He invited me to sit with him and enjoy the familiar sounds of a new day. With a bit of awkwardness, I sat down. I smiled at him, taking in the moment. Right away Floyd began to talk. I wondered how long it had been since someone sat there next to him in that chair. Floyd's eldest son was living across the country, and he hadn't seen him in over six months. His younger son, Glenn, worked nearby and came to take Floyd out to lunch or to run errands whenever he could. Glenn was an attentive and loving son, but he had his own busy career and couldn't really take the time to sit with Floyd to talk about his life and his grief. My hope was that I could fill that role and give Floyd an opportunity to share from his heart. Perhaps it was just the company, a new friend showing up to listen to his stories, but he was animated and full of life that day. He did not seem like someone who was dying.

We spent hours there, talking about how he first met Ruth when she was only sixteen, and how he thought she was so beautiful the moment he saw her smile. His words painted a vivid image of their courtship, starting with a first date to the county fair and the first kiss that "came along with a heaping pile of nerves" after their seventh date. He talked about travel, family, love, passions, faith, decorating their first home, and how he taught her to drive a truck. He and Ruth could sit in these worn wooden chairs for hours and hours, with this exact same view, same sounds, same coffee mug, day after day, and never get tired of each other.

Because this was our first visit, I arrived at Floyd's house with a clipboard filled with pages of questions attached, something I normally did for all my clients. I would rarely ask them all, but I used them to guide my conversations and find something to say if I got stuck. But after talking with Floyd that day, I realized my clipboard was still in my doula bag. I hadn't even thought about it, yet our conversation was deep and heartfelt, and we managed to talk through the things that mattered most to him.

Floyd didn't need to tell me what his passions were when he was a teenager or that he collected antique bottles. He needed to tell me that he has never stopped reaching over to the other side of the bed to touch his wife each morning, even though he knows she will not be there. He needed to tell me that he is still looking for his wife's face on those rare moments he finds himself in a crowd or walking down the grocery aisle. He needed to tell me that his heart is broken, yet he finds joy in the moments when he can share their stories. If there is any matching proportion of our love to our grief, then Floyd clearly loved Ruth with all his heart and soul. I could see it, sense it, feel it, and hear it in his gentle words.

Knowing how important it was for Floyd to remember his life with Ruth, we decided to create some legacy projects and to organize his photo collection for his two children and his grandchildren. This gave him a chance to feel productive, share stories, and still feel connected to Ruth and the memories of their life together.

One day Floyd asked me to accompany him to a doctor's appointment to take some notes, because his son wasn't available. When we arrived, Floyd walked into the office, grinning from ear to ear. I was surprised to see him so upbeat, because he was about to get an exam and some lab work, but his joy was undeniable.

The woman at the front desk looked up at us and then looked down at her keyboard.

"Patient's name?"

"My name is Floyd Barker," he said, never breaking his smile.

"Date of birth?"

"January 21, 1920."

"Reason for visit?"

Floyd began to speak, but she cut him off immediately after he said checkup and lab work.

"Go have a seat in the waiting room, please."

I noticed Floyd's demeanor had changed, yet he sat right down and looked around the waiting room. He still had a remarkable, yet somewhat less vibrant, smile of contentment on his face.

When we were called back to the examination room, we settled in, and soon a nurse arrived. Floyd greeted her with a larger-than-life smile and asked how her day was going.

"Fine, and you?" mumbled the nurse in a voice that clearly indicated she was not too interested.

"It's a lovely day and I'm doing well, thank you," Floyd beamed.

"Can you confirm your name?" asked the nurse.

"My name is Floyd Barker."

"Date of birth?"

"January 21, 1920."

"OK, I'll need to take your vitals."

We sat in silence as she took his vitals. She finished and said, "OK, the doctor will be in soon." She exited without even looking at Floyd once.

When the doctor entered, she smiled at Floyd and, with genuine care in her voice, said "Floyd, it's so good to see you. How have you been doing?"

"My body is doing as well as it can at this age, but honestly, I've really struggled with taking care of myself and keeping my routines since Ruth died. It is hard to get out of bed some days, and my morning coffee never tastes the same. I miss her so much."

The doctor looked into Floyd's eyes. "I remember when you and Ruth used to come to appointments together. You were clearly so in love and so supportive of each other. You two were such an inspiration. It must be very hard to adjust to her loss."

Floyd sighed before nodding in agreement and began telling her about how Ruth had had an impact on his life. "Everything felt so much easier when she was alive. I didn't have to think about making the bed, we would just get up and do it together as we talked. We used to walk together to the farmers market every Sunday, and now I just drive to the store when I'm running low on food. I'm trying to take care of myself, but it all feels like so much more of a chore now that I'm doing it alone."

She stood calmly and listened to his health updates, his journey with grief and loneliness, and his frustrations. She even engaged in a detailed conversation about the time he was spending on his photo collection. This compassionate doctor encouraged him to meet with friends and enjoy his life, while still allowing himself the time he needed to grieve and remember his life with Ruth.

When we left the office, Floyd looked at me with that giant, full smile on his face again. He said, "I really like her. You know, I always try to be nice to everyone, but she's the only person who ever even looks at me when I come here."

It struck me that, aside from occasional visits from his son, the outing to the doctor's office was a highlight of Floyd's week. The conversations with the intake person, the nurse, and the doctor might be the only personal interactions he would have outside of his home all week. While these brief interactions could never heal Floyd's broken heart, they could give him a chance to feel seen, heard, and cared about again.

Floyd's love for Ruth and his desire to connect with others reminded me that people and relationships are the core of what matters most. You never really know what another person is going through, or how lonely they might be. You might be the only person someone gets to see or talk to that day. Pause and listen. Take an interest in the person standing next to you. Honor them with the gift of your time, or at least with a kind smile. It's so easy.

We are all sharing the same planet.

Let's acknowledge each other.

See each other.

Listen to each other.

Even a simple smile can make someone's day.

LESSON #1

*There is a simple grace and goodness that
comes from acknowledging one another.*

One Last Time

One day, a doctor asked if I could reach out to Shawna, a sweet lady in her late sixties who had been admitted into hospice with end-stage heart failure. She was living in a room at her friend's apartment. Apparently, the friend had recently fallen in love and moved to another state, so Shawna was now living there alone. She didn't request a doula, but when the doctor asked if she wanted to talk with someone about her emotions and all she was going through, she answered with an enthusiastic yes, as if she had been invited to dinner or a concert.

Shawna and I talked on the phone for well over an hour. Our conversation covered a lot of territory and flowed like we had known each other for years. Shawna was clearly someone who enjoyed being around her friends and connecting on a deep level. She loved staying up all night talking to her roommate and hosting girls' nights for her many friends. She missed her roommate and the intimacy they shared, but she still had plenty of loving and joyful people in her life. It was important for her to spend time with them.

Shawna was feeling calm and confident she could handle things on her own at that time. She had recently started using a portable oxygen tank that she felt was helping her tremendously, and her friends were there to support her, so she was spending her limited energy enjoying time with them. We agreed to talk the next week, and then the following week, too. While we hadn't met in person, we were building a close connection. She was relieved to know I was there to talk to and to visit her when she felt like she needed someone. She planned to carry on with her routine and wanted to connect with people she loved and to live life fully, while she still could.

But as the weeks progressed, Shawna found it harder and harder to meet this goal. She became disheartened when she couldn't move freely anymore and was also tired of dragging her oxygen tank to the local coffee shop and to lunches with friends. She lay awake at night worrying about what it would be like to lose her oxygen and suffocate to death, a common fear that scared her tremendously. It was getting harder for her to breathe, and she knew that someday soon she would want to take advantage of California's End of Life Option Act and legally end her life with medication. Medical aid in dying (MAID) is becoming more and more common as people are realizing it is a compassionate and humane way for terminally ill patients to end their suffering and choose a more peaceful death.

Shawna loved life. She didn't want to die, but she didn't want to live in fear of a terrible death or be tethered to an oxygen tank, unable to breathe deeply. She was paying close attention to how she felt each day and had decided that, when the time came that she was having too much trouble breathing, was constantly feeling scared, and was unable to socialize, laugh, or leave her house, she would want to die. This is the same conscious and difficult decision all the

MAID clients I have worked with have had to make. Most were in relentless pain, were housebound, or had been dealing with terminal medical problems for a long time. When they got to a point where illness or suffering had consumed their quality of life, they chose MAID. For some people, having MAID as an option relieves their fear and anxiety, improving their quality of life, allowing them to live fully right up until the very end. MAID is a difficult decision made by a rational dying person who wants to take charge of their final moments.

Bearing witness to a MAID death is still one of the most emotional parts of my work. I don't think any of us can truly imagine what it would feel like to pick the date and time you are going to die, and then to watch the clock ticking toward that moment. Every little thing becomes more meaningful as it is being done for the last time.

This idea was articulated especially well by another MAID client of mine on the very last day of his life.

He told me he had lived differently, and with a new awareness, in his final week of life. He described it as profound and filled with poignant meaning. He explained that each day that week he paid attention to all the "lasts," which were happening constantly.

The last cup of morning coffee.

The last load of laundry.

The last chicken taco.

The last email.

The last glass of Merlot.

The last time he paid a bill.

The last phone call.

The last shower.

The last time he crawled into bed.

The last time he woke up in the morning.

The last hug.

"It's been a beautiful life, but I'm ready," he said with conviction.

With that, he slowly turned off his phone, set it on his desk, and then logged out of his computer. We both watched his screen go dark. He closed his laptop and straightened the papers on his desk. He clicked the top of his pen and put it down on a blank notepad. With the support of his walker, he stood up and slowly walked out of his office, one last time.

I know that Shawna felt this same sense of conviction and, when the time was right for her, she too picked a date. She called early one morning to see if I could be there with her later that week when she would take the medication. It would be the first time we would meet in person. Her family would be there, too, and she thought they could use some support. I promised to be there at the scheduled time, two days away.

That afternoon Shawna called me again. "Sorry to bother you, but is there any chance you could come over? I'm having a hard time breathing. I've already called the hospice nurse, but I want to talk, and I would love to see you."

I was so grateful she felt comfortable calling, and headed right to her house. Her breathing was more labored than it had been in the past, and she seemed frightened, but we were able to talk about MAID and planned for the days ahead. She told me about her friends and family, who would all be there the next day for a final get-together. She was looking forward to that.

During our two-hour visit, I asked twice if she wanted me to spend the night with her so she didn't have to be alone. She said no both times. When I was getting ready to leave, we reconfirmed the time I would return two days later. I told her I would keep my phone close that night so she could call if she needed me.

We said goodbye, and, just as I turned the creaky knob on the front door, she said, "Diane, would you *really* be willing to spend the night?"

"Of course, I would be honored to stay here with you tonight," I told her. I ran home for some food and supplies and returned by eight o'clock that evening.

Doulas always show up prepared. I brought my own pillow, blanket, water bottle, phone charger, snacks, and everything I needed for a sleepover. She was tired and showed me to the room across from hers where I could stay. The first thing I noticed was a framed photo of Shawna and her roommate laughing in a café, a reminder of days past. I paused and wondered what it had been like the last time they shared that type of big, joyful laughter together . . . if it had been in a café like in the photo, or out surrounded by a big group of friends, or right here in this bedroom. Friendship clearly meant a lot to Shawna.

She thanked me for being there and said, "I won't need anything. I just feel better knowing you're here in case of an emergency. Don't worry if you hear any coughing, choking, or gagging. It happens all the time. And I may get up to use the bathroom. Don't get up if you hear me shuffling. I can do everything on my own. I'll call for you if I need anything."

She rumbled around her bedroom and finally settled down in bed and quickly fell asleep. I must have fallen asleep as well because I woke up to a soft voice in my room: "Diane, are you awake? Can I come in?"

"Of course. Come on in," I said as I quickly sat up.

"I'm fine. I'm fine. Everything's good. Sorry to bother you. I was just wondering if you'd ever been to a concert at the Cow Palace?"

"Oh yes! A bunch of times. I saw Elton John, Fleetwood Mac, Journey, and lots of my favorite bands there when I was younger," I shared without pausing to consider the odd timing of that question.

She sat on the end of my bed for twenty minutes, sharing stories about past concerts she attended and her love for music, until she got short of breath and said, "I think I have to stop talking, but I don't want to. This is so much fun."

I encouraged her to go back to her room and get some sleep, which she did.

A little later, I heard her getting out of bed again. I listened as she passed the bathroom and came toward my room, step by step. Again, she said, "Diane, are you awake? Sorry to bother you, but can I come in?"

"Of course. Come on in," I said as I quickly sat up again.

"Do you ever wonder what it will be like to die? I've been thinking about that a lot more now that I know it's coming soon."

We talked for an hour about her fears, her worries, and her family. We talked about love, loss, marriage, grief, and how much fun girlfriends are. And then she went back to bed. I sat in the dark for a long time, contemplating the reality that this was the last time Shawna would have a chance for a sleepover with a friend.

Shawna slept for about three hours. I was awake reading a book with the light from my phone when I heard her get up again. This time she went into the bathroom, but then she poked her head into my room. "You're awake," she said enthusiastically.

This time we talked about her regrets, some mistakes she made over the years, and a friend that she had lost contact with whom she had decided to call that day. We talked about forgiveness, her children, her spiritual practice, and how she felt at peace with her beliefs.

Shawna thanked me for being there and told me that, if she knew we would have had so much fun together, she would have invited me over weeks ago. She was sad that this would be her last night to talk and laugh with a friend. We smiled at each other with that knowing look, and she went back to her room and fell fast asleep until close to noon, waking up just in time for her family's arrival.

When I showed up the next day, Shawna was calm. She told me that she felt unburdened and free. She hadn't realized that she had bottled up so many emotions, even the good ones. She said that, even though her body was dying, and her breathing was worse, she felt fully alive that morning for the first time in months.

Looking back, I realize that night I spent with Shawna gave her one last time for a sleepover, for laughter, for a deep conversation, and for one more normal moment with a friend. She inspired me not to take anything for granted, not even the simplest moments.

What if we all lived as if each day were our last day? How would it change the way we show up in the world? How would it make us be more mindful about being present?

Our last sunrise.

Our last sunset.

Our last hug.

What would you be grateful for?

What would you do differently?

Every moment is a gift. Tomorrow is not guaranteed. Be present. Take it all in. You never know when it will be the very last time.

LESSON #2

When we live each day as if it were our last, we begin to cherish the beauty of life around us.

Damn, You're Beautiful

Have you ever canceled a date because of a pimple? Or cried because of a bad haircut? Have you ever felt insecure about going out with friends because you've gained some weight or because you've added a few wrinkles to your beautiful face? I know I have, and when I look back, I'm a bit embarrassed at how shallow and self-critical I've been over the years. I suppose it's a regret, because I wish I had learned to love myself sooner.

We judge ourselves so harshly. Our perceived imperfections tend to glare at us in the mirror, bullying us, telling us lies, and causing us to see only faults and flaws. I have heard too many clients say, "I've hated my body my entire life." It breaks my heart to hear, but I can relate. I've spent decades hiding certain body parts and judging myself in ways that I would never judge anyone else. Then breast cancer came along and challenged everything about how I saw myself. Instantly, those body parts became allies in my journey toward acceptance, healing, understanding what I truly care about, and cherishing that which makes me feel whole.

The first time I ever felt beautiful was shortly after my double mastectomy. My breasts were gone, replaced by scars that molded into my rib cage. I was bald and skinny, and my eyes were sunken. Chemo caused my stomach to bloat, and my face was covered in a bumpy, red rash. People stared at me and my three young children with pity, and even though my sweet husband held me tightly, rubbed my bald head, and told me I was beautiful every single day, it didn't help me feel better. I felt ugly and a bit scary looking . . . until one tender moment.

For some unexplainable reason, in the middle of a sleepless night, on my way to the bathroom, I looked at myself in the mirror and saw my beauty. I just stood there, naked and alone, with my bright red scars and my big blue eyes looking back at me in the mirror. I felt strong, confident, and overcome with a sense of awe at the amazing miracle of my body's unwavering determination to heal itself. There was something about me that was glowing, like the light from within me was so much brighter than anything that might look like darkness on the outside. My heart filled with self-compassion, and my mind expanded to make space for a new way of treating myself . . . with radical kindness and acceptance.

That realization stuck with me and changed the way I looked at myself and the world around me in the tough months that followed. One day, between chemo treatments, I pulled out some old photos and spent the day organizing albums and writing notes on the back of each photo for my kids to help them remember all the good times we shared together. Some of the photos were faded. Some were blurry. Some were stained and curled with age. Time had erased some memories, but others were as clear as yesterday. Most of the time I was smiling, but I also recall being preoccupied with my weight, my outfit, or whatever flaws I felt were going to be permanently memorialized in each snapshot. I missed many moments, and many opportunities, because I didn't accept or love myself. But as I stared at these photos, there was a reality that hit me with a new awareness and sense of self-compassion. I was always beautiful. I just couldn't see it.

I know that I would have missed many more moments in my life if I had not had that epiphany in the middle of the night. Perhaps I would have been too embarrassed or insecure to join in on social gatherings because of my physical appearance after my mastectomy. I would have hidden myself away to avoid the sad stares from strangers, rather than having the courage to step out and be authentic and alive.

We cannot let our harsh inner critic and our personal judgments about our physical appearance stop us from living a full and vibrant life. My whole life I thought that knowing you were beautiful was only for people who looked a certain way, like models or those who were just "objectively beautiful." We're all beautiful. It's just so hard to see it in ourselves sometimes.

Maybe I would have been able to see my own beauty sooner if I had been introduced to someone like Drew Foster.

Drew was born beautiful, in his own unique way, and he embraced it. He was also born with two rare diseases. The first was osteogenesis imperfecta, a brittle bone disease that was diagnosed in utero. Drew had already suffered six broken bones before he was even born. His parents knew Drew would be a fragile boy, but what nobody knew until Drew was born was that he also had a rare disease called neurocutaneous hypermelanosis, a disorder that affects the central nervous system and can cause a massive number of birthmarks all over the body. He was born covered with large and small brown birthmarks from head to toe. Even Drew's brain was covered in birthmarks. At the time he was born, Drew was the only known documented case of a person born with both conditions at the same time.

I learned of Drew through a dear friend and colleague of mine, Angela Shook, a death doula who was working with Children's Miracle Network in Michigan when she met Drew and his family. Outside of being a support for them, Angela was Drew's close friend. She saw the playful glimmer in his eye and knew right away that he was an old soul. He had such enthusiasm for meeting new people. At the age of five, the first thing he said to Angela was, "Wassup? You wanna hang out?"

One year Drew was chosen as the "champion" of the Children's Miracle Network. Along with countless photo ops and social engagements, he was awarded a trip to Disneyland with the other champions and their families from around the country. Angela accompanied them on the trip. When they got to Disneyland, Drew met with several celebrities, and had a special visit with the Jonas Brothers. This was only one of the many adventures in Drew's exciting life.

From his power wheelchair, he learned how to hunt and fish. In 2007, Drew went to the White House and met George W. Bush. He hung out with NFL and NBA players and mingled with a long list of celebrities and athletes. He was the guest of honor at the 2011 Miss America pageant. Even with all the beautiful women in the room that night, it was Drew who stole everybody's heart. He wasn't star-struck, and graciously greeted them all and posed for photos, as if he knew that he was the real star.

Drew could've had a completely different life. He could've been kept at home or isolated for fear of breaking his bones, but Drew's parents, whom Angela credits for his amazing spirit, had a different dream for him. They wanted Drew to experience life, and they gave him every opportunity to do so. Drew grew up knowing he was different and that his lifespan would be limited. He knew he would never grow to be tall and would always be covered in dark spots. He knew he was fragile and always at risk. But that didn't stop him. Drew said on more than one occasion that, spots and broken bones and all, he wouldn't change any of it! He squeezed more into his short life than many of us ever will.

Even though we never truly know exactly what another person feels, Drew just never seemed to struggle with confidence. Maybe there were some self-doubts, but they rarely showed. Mostly, he just loved himself.

One night, Drew was excited to go to one of his favorite Japanese restaurants for dinner with Angela. It was a hibachi-style place where you sit at a community table and the chef cooks your food right in front of you. Angela and Drew were settling in at the table when they overheard someone who was about to join them say, "Ew, I don't want to sit next to him."

Angela was outraged, but Drew was used to it. He looked at Angela as if to tell her, "I've got this."

Then Drew looked over at the woman and said, "But I'm so cool! I look good! I'm so much fun. What's your problem?" He liked to tell people, "Look for the happy spots in your life!" (A joke in honor of his birthmarks, but it got the point across.)

According to Angela, "He was beautiful, unique, and awesome because he was just Drew. He could never be anybody else, and there would never be another person like him, and he reveled in that." She liked to say to him, "Nobody could ever be as cool as you, 'cause you are just the Drewest most Drewest person in the whole wide world."

Even though some people stared, Drew gathered a crowd around him wherever he went. People were attracted to him. He was just over three feet tall, drove an electric wheelchair, and didn't look like anyone else. He had a smile that would light up the room, and he always had an amazing sense of humor.

Along with the good times, Angela showed up for the hard times, too. She supported him through many treatments and surgeries. As he grew older, they often texted each other in the middle of a sleepless night. Sometimes they talked about death and dying, and Drew shared his hope about helping others, maybe even becoming a death doula himself one day.

On Angela's wedding day, she danced with her dad, and then with her husband, and then it was Drew's turn. He had a special dance with just Angela at first, but soon her bridesmaids surrounded them, and they all danced together in the center of the room.

"Once again, you stole the show," Angela said to Drew later that night.

Drew smiled and said, "I hope nobody will ever forget me."

"Nobody ever will," Angela agreed with a laugh.

Drew died at age twenty-three, after a short but action-packed life. Angela remembered what Drew had said at her wedding and she thought to herself, "No one will ever forget you, Drew, especially me."

When I first heard Drew's story, I immediately found myself thinking about that night, standing in front of the bathroom mirror, and how long it took me to finally see my own beauty. My wish for you is that it doesn't take a health crisis for you to allow yourself to be beautiful.

Don't wait until you are on your deathbed to love and accept yourself. Do it now. You are beautiful. It's your perspective that determines how much you will see yourself shine, both inside and out.

LESSON #3

You are already beautiful.

Knocking on Ellie's Door

We often race through our lives without truly pausing to consider where we are even going. Why do we rush? Why are we in such a hurry? When you hurry, you pass by the present moment on your way to the next one. Learning to pause can change your life.

Being still and taking a long pause can be a golden opportunity for us to regroup and make thoughtful, informed decisions. Psychologist Viktor Frankl taught us there is a space between the stimulus and the response, and *that* is where our power lies. The space can be an instant or an intentionally long time, but this is when you are aware and contemplating, rather than doing. You don't always get to choose what happens to you in life, but your reaction to what happens is up to you. It starts with slowing down, paying attention, and giving yourself permission to hit the pause button and be still from time to time, even if it's only for one minute a day.

Soon after I completed my cancer treatments and graduated with my master's degree, I began volunteering at a local hospice, where I met Ellie, a young mom with three children, who only a month earlier had been diagnosed with metastatic breast cancer. Because I was a recent breast cancer survivor with three young children myself, it was ironic that Ellie was one of my first hospice clients. She was diagnosed early with breast cancer, which was followed by surgery and chemo, only to have the cancer return and take over her body with a vengeance. Her story tugged at my heart and caused me to deeply examine the shadows and triggers that might affect my ability to be a death doula. I couldn't help but recall my own story, and my own worries about a possible reoccurrence of cancer. I needed to put aside my own fears to fully be there for her and her family. I thought seriously about whether I could handle the emotions that would continue to surface, and I decided to take that first and most difficult step. I showed up.

After pulling into Ellie's driveway, I said a silent prayer to release my own tension, worries, troubles, and fears. Then I knocked on Ellie's door. I heard dogs barking and children scurrying around and realized that, along with the story of Ellie's cancer, there was a full life playing out on the other side of the door. Everyone knew Ellie was dying, but that day Ellie was living, and she would be living every day until the last.

Ellie told me right away that she could not sit still, that she hadn't had the patience to read a book in years, and that she had left a giant trail of dust behind her as she "went zipping through life like a roadrunner." She admitted she had never paused in her entire life. She had a lot of questions and wanted to talk about dying, but she also didn't want it to interfere with her living.

This was confirmed when Ellie revealed that she had a long list of things she needed to get done before she died. This list included painting some furniture, making fresh fruit jam for her neighbors

and friends, and finally finishing a scarf that she'd begun knitting almost a decade earlier. There were upcoming parent-teacher meetings, social gatherings, and even a small vacation to celebrate her
twelfth wedding anniversary. Ellie was active and fully alive. Other
than her bald head and a slow shuffle, you would never have known
she was dying.

With Ellie, I used one of the foundations of doula work—I began
our relationship by meeting her exactly where she was, in this case,
by diving right into the chaos with her. This was Ellie's journey, and
it was important for our relationship that I meet her in that chaos
with curiosity, respect, and acceptance. We built our trust based on
her needs at that time, which were clearly to, as she said, "get this
shit done!" And so, we got it done . . . together.

Our weekly meetings involved having deep conversations while I
followed her around the house. We spent time working on her projects, organizing kitchen cupboards, pulling weeds, and talking about
her hopes and dreams. This went on for months, and, nestled between her frantic to-do list, we also managed to create a legacy garden for her children and talk about some of the more meaningful
things she might want to consider as time went on.

As with most clients, when the disease progressed, Ellie naturally
began to slow down and have less energy for the tasks she wanted to
complete. The cancer, now in her bones, was rapidly forcing her to
remove items from her long and detailed list. Over time, Ellie made
peace with her limitations, and she began to pause and go inward.
This is a beautiful place to be, that transitional time when the external world starts to be less inviting, and the internal world is calling
out for attention. There is powerful work to be done during this

time, and even as a new hospice volunteer, the shift was impossible for me to miss. As Ellie began to pause, I paused with her.

The time had come for Ellie to contemplate her final days. The jam was made, the scarf was knitted, and it was time for Ellie to shift away from those tasks of everyday life and to pause.

The pause is where wisdom lives and growth happens. This window of time, no matter how brief, makes space for the truth, and the truth brings opportunities for peace, closure, comfort, and an understanding of what might be left to do.

We finally narrowed down the questions she had been pondering and explored the ones that were most meaningful to her:

Have I lived a good life?

Have I been a good person?

Did I make a difference?

Was I loved and did I love back?

Was I kind?

While it took two months, countless conversations, and lots of time to pause and reflect, Ellie finally came to a place of peace. I remember particularly one thoughtful and calm afternoon that Ellie and I shared, when she was able to pause, look around at her house, and notice what all of her effort added up to. The jam on the windowsill wasn't just a sweet treat, it was the love and nourishment that she had always poured into her community. The painted furniture wasn't just seating, it represented the comfort and support that she provided to uplift the people around her. She saw the scarf and felt all the warmth and care she wrapped her kids up in. During this brief pause we shared, she saw not the tasks she had accomplished but the beautiful and vibrant life that she had built up around her.

Ellie realized that she had lived a full and meaningful life. She could answer the most important questions with clarity and a soft smile. She felt like her life mattered, that she mattered. She loved deeply and was loved in return. She would be remembered as a compassionate person who cared about others.

She was sad, but ready to let go.

Ellie died on a warm spring day, surrounded by love. Wildflowers were blooming outside her bedroom window next to her flourishing children's legacy garden. Jars of fresh strawberry jam were lined up on her kitchen counter to be shared with family, friends, and neighbors. In my pocket was a letter she had written for her husband, which I was instructed to leave with him after she died. She was ready. She did her work. She lived fully and she died in peace.

Her life and her story have guided me to hundreds of other front doors over the years, where I always pause, say a silent prayer to release my own tension, worries, troubles, and fears, and then knock softly on the door, never knowing what story is unfolding on the other side. I've come to look forward to that unknown. It keeps me curious and open.

This skill of knowing how to pause gave me strength and a sense of calm about continuing to work with the dying. It has also made a difference in how I show up for my friends and family, and for a stranger at the grocery store.

If not for Ellie, I would not have learned how to separate my own stories from everyone else's story. Their story is theirs, not mine. Their journey is theirs, not mine. And my job is not to carry the burdens and fears of others. My job is to listen, be present for all the emotions in the room, and to support each client on their journey toward acceptance and peace. When I give myself a moment to pause, I remember this, and I can move forward with ease.

If you are having trouble pausing, I suggest you find one thing every day that strikes you as beautiful and look at it closely for a full minute. It can be the face of a grandchild, a breathtaking view, or a slice of buttered toast. Just soak it in.

This moment allows you to hit the pause button on your active life and reflect on what matters most. I've learned that sometimes even one minute of stillness can help shift someone's day.

Being still might cause you to contemplate not only *what* you are doing with your time but also *why* you are doing the things you do.

Our choices become clearer when we pause to understand them. Whether it's a simple decision or a life-changing one, you will gain wisdom in those quiet moments between the stimulus and the response.

Like with Ellie, pausing empowers us to find purpose, even in our everyday lives.

Slow down.

Give yourself time to be still.

Get curious about what might be waiting for you in the silence of a pause.

LESSON #4

There is power in an intentional pause.

You Are Not Fine

Most of us have experienced sleepless nights at some point in our lives. We might lie in bed contemplating the end of a relationship, a job transition, our physical health, concerns about children and family members, or countless other issues that tug on us. Then, the next morning, most of us wake up and get back to life again.

We stop for our morning coffee. The barista asks, "How are you doing today?"

"I'm fine," we say automatically.

We head to our job, to the bank, for an appointment, or off to see some friends. All along the way, whenever someone asks how we are doing, we repeat the same hollow answer: "I'm fine."

But are we all really fine? Are *you* fine? In our stressful, fast-paced world, it seems that we are all filled with so many emotions, and so many worries, that I wonder if any of us are ever simply "fine." We are complex beings, and taking the time to ask ourselves how we are truly feeling gives us a chance to pay attention to all the emotions that may be percolating within us.

So why do we avoid sharing the truth about how we are doing?

Perhaps we don't want to pass our problems off to others, or maybe we don't want to be judged for having problems at all. Maybe we don't want others to worry about us, but that takes away an opportunity to be loved and to allow others to share their love as well. Being an authentic human being comes with a wide range of emotions, and to name them is a powerful skill.

Some emotions are harder to cope with. Anger and fear can feel immediate and demanding. It might trigger a physical fight-or-flight response and is often the cause of great anxiety. While fear has played an important role in survival throughout our evolution, it can also be emotionally debilitating and distressing, especially at the end of one's life. However, tucked deep inside a fear, or a worry, there may be an opportunity to heal and grow.

I'm often called in to help with the many common fears that come up for my clients. Dying is a raw and real experience. There's no time for hiding and denying what's in your heart and on your mind. It's time for pure truth, so it's helpful to say it out loud to identify what's causing those sleepless nights. A significant part of my job is to find ways to create comfort and peace. The good news is, when I hear about someone's worries, I know where to start. My clients are never just "fine," so I always ask them, "What do you worry about when you are lying awake in bed at night?"

Here are some of the answers they have shared with me:

> "I'm so worried about my young children. There is still so much I want to teach them. Will they be OK? I'm not totally sure they will. I hope so."
> *Mandy, age 42*

"I'm not afraid of dying, but I am afraid of all the pain and suffering that might happen."   *Ezra, age 79*

"I lay in bed at night thinking of the giant task of preparing to die. I've handled all the bills and paperwork for thirty-five years. I keep trying to remember if all my documents and affairs are in order. My husband will be going through enough changes and emotions when I die. I don't want him to have to deal with this stuff, along with having to live alone."   *Lowell, age 78*

"I'm worried that my spiritual practice hasn't gone deep enough. I feel like I've been searching for a spiritual foundation my entire life and I'm still not 100 percent sure what I believe, and that scares me."   *Robin, age 71*

"I don't want to be alone."   *Jenna, age 58*

Worries come in a variety of shapes and sizes. Sometimes we say them out loud, but most often we keep them hidden. Some people hold their worries tightly to their chest, even with a large community of support. Roger was one of those people. He said he was "fine," but he was clearly unsettled. He thought he was hiding it well, but his family knew better.

Roger was an eighty-year-old retired dairy rancher dying of lung cancer. His daughter, Jessie, called us because she felt her father was "bottled up and twisted" and telling everyone he was "fine" when everyone knew the truth. He was dying, and he was hiding his pain and suffering. Jessie's message sounded urgent, yet the urgency was not about his impending death but rather his emotional state.

Over the phone, Jessie told me about her dad, getting right to the heart of her concerns. "He's been stoic his entire life, beginning with his childhood that included an endless rotation of foster care families. My dad had very little consistency and no unconditional love in his life until he married my mom, Julie. They've now been married fifty-five years and have five children and thirteen grandchildren. They were enjoying a peaceful retirement in a small, rural farming town with all of us close by, but then my dad got sick."

She told me that Roger's early life had been a forbidden topic that was never discussed in the home and that her parents had a rather unaffectionate relationship, even though they loved each other deeply. She said Roger was a good father, and treated Julie with respect, but he never really shared his emotions freely. It suddenly occurred to her that maybe her father was holding a lifetime of feelings, not just about his current situation but about his entire past, including his childhood.

She explained that her dad had softened over the years, especially when the grandkids came along, but lately he was less affectionate toward them, unusually closed-off, and grumpy. She was frustrated and they were all tired of him saying he was always "good" or "fine." Like many families who call doulas, she thought that "maybe an unrelated outsider would give him the freedom to talk about his feelings and his fears about death and dying."

I told her about the work we do and asked her to talk to her dad to see if he would be interested in meeting with an end-of-life doula.

"I thought you were a death doula?" she asked, looking for some clarification.

"Most people know us as death doulas, but I usually prefer to call myself an end-of-life doula. Most of our clients work with us from the time of diagnosis all the way until their death. Some curious people call us when they are young and healthy, just wanting to be informed and plan ahead. Others call us after a terminal illness begins to impact the quality of their life, and they want to talk about how to live well, and how to die well, too. Some call us to sit vigil at their bedside, with just days or hours left to live. But whenever they call, I always remember that people are whole and living up until the very end. Death is just one moment of one day. All the days before death are filled with an opportunity for love, healing, growth, and connection, even if that simply means holding someone's hand. I also think *end-of-life doula* is a gentler term for those who struggle with having these hard conversations."

"I think my dad will respond much better to that. I'll talk to him this evening."

I was surprised when Roger called me back himself the very next day. "My daughter said I needed to call you because my family is worried about me. I'm fine. They don't need to worry about me."

"I think they really care about you and want to be sure you are able to talk about all that you're going through with someone," I explained.

"I know. I know. I just don't want to worry them. They can't handle seeing me like this, and there's nothing they can do about it anyway. My wife gets hysterical just watching me try to get my aching body out of bed in the morning. Then the days just seem to get more emotional every hour until Jessie comes over, and then she gets all emotional, too. I'm just tired." Roger surprisingly volunteered a lot of information.

It reminded me there are always at least two perspectives. Roger wasn't sharing his emotions with his family, but he was also trying to protect his own limited energy for the precious time he had left, and he had every right to be holding back to avoid worrying his family.

This is a classic story. Roger wasn't saying anything about his illness and pain because he didn't want to worry his family, but they were worried because Roger wasn't saying anything about his illness and pain. It's the unhelpful cycle of each person protecting the other person, when what they really need is a healthy conversation, a realistic plan, some togetherness, and probably a good cry. These dynamics are rooted in love and care, but they can stifle communication and hide the truth.

Roger and I agreed to meet each other a few days later. When I arrived, he opened the door and ushered me into the family room. While he excused himself to use the bathroom, I sat and looked around the room, taking in the wall across from me, covered entirely with a lifetime of family photos. It struck me in that moment that the photos we display for others to see do not capture all that comes together to make a life. As in most homes, the photos on Roger's wall were filled with smiles, vacations, weddings, holiday celebrations, and family gatherings. We don't tend to display the hard times . . . no grief-stricken faces, no hospital stays, no divorce papers. Perhaps we want to remember only the good times, but if I'm going to get to know a client, I want to hear the stories that live between the smiling faces hanging on the wall. We never really know a person until we take the time to hear their story . . . the full, true story . . . including the parts that didn't make it into a picture frame.

Given Roger's reported history of not wanting to go deep, I started by asking my least favorite basic question. "How are you doing today, Roger?"

"I'm fine. I'm fine," he said. "Everything's good over here. The girls are out, so it's just you and me. So, what do you want to talk about?"

Two hours passed. As I supported him with some thoughtful questions, curiosity, and a warm heart willing to simply listen, Roger slowly opened up and shared his life with me, starting with his "lonely and emotionless childhood." We explored the dynamics that were embedded in his current relationships and his family, with Roger accustomed to always being the person who was in control, strong, and unshakable.

During our conversation, some of his needs were revealed. I asked him, "Roger, what's bothering you the most?"

He responded clearly, "Everyone treats me like I'm already dead. They talk about me like I'm not in the room and keep me out of family decisions. It makes me feel like nobody needs me anymore."

Roger's voice was cracking as he continued, "And I don't always want to talk about cancer. I want some alone time. I want my wife to relax and watch a movie with me. I don't need a lot, but everyone seems to be buzzing around me like I'm helpless and dying . . . OK, I'm dying, but not today! I would just like the days to be normal again."

We talked about what changes could be made to make him feel like part of the family again. He simply wanted to participate in the chores and to be needed. "They follow me around and try to brush my hair and make the bed every time I get up to pee. This may sound crazy, but I haven't even changed the toilet paper roll in months. Every time it's almost empty, someone replaces it, like I can't even do that. I can brush my own damn hair and change the toilet paper roll, too!"

That conversation led to a family meeting that was centered in truth and gave Roger a chance to finally voice his frustrations. He admitted that he was not "fine" and asked clearly for what he wanted. Over time, the entire family was able to verbalize their needs and find ways to keep living life without the dark cloud of cancer taking over every waking moment. And because of the honesty, Roger was able to step back into his favorite roles of husband, father, grandfather, and rancher.

My work was eventually done, although Roger wanted to keep meeting every couple of weeks for some legacy work. He wanted to leave his wife a special gift. Decades ago, she lost her wedding ring. They replaced it with a new and slightly bigger diamond. Years later, they found the original ring stuck in a crack in the back of a large wooden dresser drawer. The ring sat in a box for years until Roger had the idea to surprise her with a gift. He took the ring to a jeweler, had the stone removed, and made it into a necklace for her, surrounded with eighteen smaller stones to represent their five children and thirteen grandchildren. He wanted this to be a gift for Julie after his death, along with a heartwarming love letter. We worked on the letter together over a few visits and talked about his beautiful and challenging life. I learned a lot about those spaces between the smiling faces in the photos that lined their walls.

A few weeks later, Jessie called me. "My dad isn't doing too great. He is coughing nonstop and is short of breath. He asked if you would come by and see him." I said yes and suggested she contact the hospice nurse, too.

As I drove toward Roger's house, I felt peaceful and full. What an honor it is to be invited into such an intimate and meaningful time in a person's life.

Jessie saw me through the kitchen window and rushed out to let me in. She was calm, yet I could see the worry and fear in her eyes. "I'm scared he's going to choke to death. Thanks for the advice to call the nurse. He's coming over within the hour."

I walked into Roger's room and saw he was struggling, but he smiled and waved me toward him. "Go ahead and ask me," he challenged.

"How are you doing today, Roger?" I asked him with a slight smirk on my face, because I knew he had learned to tell the truth about how he feels.

"I feel like shit!" he replied with a crackly but clear voice, followed by his trademark grin.

Soon the hospice nurse came and took Roger's vitals, adjusted his oxygen, and put a plan in place to monitor and control his pain. The hospice nurse promised to return the next day, but there was no need. Roger died that night, with his family by his side.

I pay very close attention to the honest, thoughtful words my clients use to describe how they are feeling. They tell me they are rested, scared, introspective, grateful, peaceful, irritated, struggling, worried, calm, hopeful, and more. They are never just *fine*—because no one is just *fine* these days. We are all so much more than that.

We can learn a lot from Roger. There's a lot going on emotionally inside all of us. Feel your feelings. All of them. It's OK to feel sad, mad, scared, angry, or any other emotion that might be brewing inside you. Once you identify an emotion you are experiencing, you can dig a little deeper by asking yourself why you might be feeling that way.

Part of being authentic and getting to know yourself starts with how you answer the most frequently asked question, "How are you?" We often robotically respond with words like *fine*, *OK*, or *good*. Those words have no depth and don't tell us anything at all. Next time someone asks, "How are you?" take a moment to pause, think about it, and tell them the truth. It builds deeper relationships and gives you a moment to check in with yourself, too.

LESSON #5

There is a freedom in being honest about how we are feeling, even if it isn't always positive.

All Big Things

Do you ever dwell on something you did that you just can't let go of? Maybe it was something small or something that didn't even feel that bad when you did it, like telling a small lie, littering, sneaking food, or calling in sick when you were feeling just fine. I've done plenty of things in my life I'm not proud of, and some of these things, even though they seem rather trivial, still take up space in my heart and mind.

Once I told a health-conscious boyfriend that I would make two fresh homemade pumpkin pies for our Thanksgiving feast with friends. I tried, but when I saw that the baked pumpkin had turned to mush, I threw it down the garbage disposal and quickly ran to the grocery store to buy two cans of the highly processed yet dependably thick and tasty pumpkin pie mix. After returning home, I got even more sneaky by leaving the colorful, charred pumpkin rinds on the counter while I grabbed the empty pumpkin pie mix cans and a shovel, and found the perfect spot to bury the cans outside. I continued making the pies, with the fresh smell of the pumpkin filling the house when my boyfriend returned. It took everything I had to control the grin on my face later that night when he asked for a second slice, but years later I started to feel bad about the whole sneaky thing.

It might seem like a small thing to get stuck on, but after working with the dying for so many years, I know better. I've heard such stories repeatedly. One client called his neighbor before he died to apologize for repeatedly helping himself to eggs from the neighbor's chicken coop. Another client still remembered and deeply regretted stealing her classmate's lunches in third grade. Another still felt terrible for shutting the door on a young man who had finally built up the courage to come to her house and ask her out. When someone is close to death, sometimes the little things become the big things. And sometimes, after the seemingly little things are addressed, there is more room to take a deep, hard look at the bigger things, something my young client Carrie quickly found out.

Carrie was only thirty-six and dying of a rare cancer. It was stage IV, inoperable, and aggressive. She was diagnosed just two months before I met her. During our first visit, she told me she immediately moved to the San Francisco Bay Area from Wisconsin after receiving her diagnosis, leaving her parents, sister, and friends behind. Though the doctors had told her she had only a few months left to live, she wanted to be with a man she loved and wanted to seek alternative medical advice and some spiritual healing. She was glowing, vibrant, energetic, and beautiful. From her outer appearance, you would never have imagined she was sick.

She was optimistic and focused on "winning the battle" with cancer. She was determined and had appointments lined up every day for two weeks. She had doctor's visits at Stanford University Medical Center, lymphatic massages, vitamin infusions, meditations with her spiritual teacher, and healing circles planned at a retreat center. But even so, serious illnesses have a way of making us stop and reflect upon our lives. She still was planning to "win the battle" with her cancer, but she liked the idea of healing emotionally as well as physically and thought this cancer diagnosis and time in California offered her the perfect opportunity for a fresh start. Carrie began contemplating what might be left to do so that she could have a clean slate.

During our second visit she shared story after story about "the little things" that were on her mind. She wanted to apologize to her boyfriend for being so distant and short-tempered recently. She wanted to find a couple from whom she rented a room years ago but never paid. She'd withheld her rent money because she thought they'd been unfair to her, but over the years, she realized they'd been reasonable and even showed compassion to her during a hard time.

She told me she felt bad about the times she snuck out at night to sleep at her boyfriend's house when she was a teenager. How she put a different code on a bag of fancy cashews at a grocery store one time because she thought they were too expensive. How she once lied to a cop when she got pulled over, and how she returned many summer dresses to the department store after wearing them out to parties. She laughed that day at some of her sillier stories, yet as I was preparing to leave, she told me that a giant weight had been lifted and she hadn't realized she was holding all those stories inside, even the little ones. It felt like she was opening up, yet I sensed there were many more layers to her unfolding life story. And as it turns out, there were.

The third visit was different from the moment Carrie answered the door. She was moving slowly and told me she was feeling emotional. I sat next to her on the couch, and the tears immediately began to flow. She looked me in the eyes and said, "I'm dying . . . *and* I'm a terrible mother."

I looked back into her eyes, taking it all in, and holding silent space for all the emotions to arise and for whatever words wanted to come next.

"I didn't tell you the whole story last week," she said, and continued crying. The part she left out was that she had two teenage children who were living with their dad in Wisconsin. Years earlier, she had met a man named Robert in California and decided to separate from her husband and distance herself from her children, going to California for longer and longer periods of time to be with Robert.

"I chose romance, sex, wine country dinners, and exotic vacations over raising my kids and being there to watch them grow up. I've been so selfish. I've been torn apart with my heart in two places, and I've destroyed my relationship with my daughters. I figured I had time to make it up to them. And now it's too late. I won't get to see them graduate from college, or even high school. I won't see them get married, and I will never meet my grandkids. I will never see them decorate their first home, and I won't be there to hold them through the hard times."

She paused and looked right back into my eyes. "And it's worse than that. Perhaps I could accept the future, if only I had chosen a different past." She looked out the window into the green fields as if she were hoping her girls would come running toward her, but she knew better.

"They have not been my priority. We've grown apart, and sometimes when I'm in Wisconsin, they are too busy to spend time with me. And I get it. It's my fault."

Carrie wondered if she could ever forgive herself, but more important, she wondered if she could make amends and if her daughters could ever forgive her.

Unfortunately, Carrie's health began to decline. She was losing weight and sleeping more, and her abundant enthusiasm and energy were beginning to wane. I knew the window of opportunity was closing, yet she was still unwilling to tell her children she was dying, or to go and see them. Carrie knew she couldn't make up for lost time, but she could at least leave her daughters something to remember her by. Though it would not have been my choice, a doula meets the client where they are, and I respected her wishes to plan a legacy from afar.

Carrie wanted to write letters to her daughters so they could get to know who she was over the years as well as have a reminder of her during their birthdays and special moments in their lives. Together, we decorated two shoeboxes with light yellow wrapping paper and pasted on inspiring words cut from magazines that were piled on her nightstand. She wrote her daughters' names, Angie and Lane, in beautiful cursive writing on the tops of each box. She sealed poems, photos, recipes, and some of her favorite earrings and bracelets into the growing pile of envelopes. For their birthdays, she wrote to them about who she was, how she celebrated, and what her life was like when she was twenty-one, twenty-five, thirty, and thirty-five. I could see these letter boxes were filling Carrie's life, and her time, with meaning.

Carrie also methodically went through her clothes, jewelry, and all her personal possessions to pick her favorite items and set them aside with notes to her daughters about why they meant so much to her. She wrote notes on the backs of the photos she had framed on her dresser. She picked out special gifts to give them for the coming Christmas, even though she knew she would not likely be there to give them herself. She cried through each session, and each time when I asked her if she felt like reaching out to her children or going back to Wisconsin to see them, she said no.

Eventually, Carrie decided to stop receiving medical treatments, and enrolled in hospice. She was still living her life and finding some moments of joy, but she was acutely aware of her bloated abdomen, the dark circles under her eyes, the increasing and debilitating pain, and the limits on her energy and mobility. Even her spiritual teacher had given her a sense that the healing might come after she was released from the pain and suffering she was experiencing in her life, both emotional and physical.

One day I asked her, "What do you worry about in the middle of the night?"

She gazed back out into that same field of green, as if she could see all the way to Wisconsin. "I worry that I will never see my kids again. I worry they will hate me forever and that they will think I never loved them. They won't know how sorry I am for the decisions I made, or how proud I am of their generous hearts, or how much goodness they have added to my life. When I lay in bed at night, I imagine hugging them, and I worry I will never get that chance."

Two days later, I got a call from Carrie. She was in Wisconsin.

Three weeks later, she died in the arms of her teenage children.

Carrie had the courage to say she was sorry and to make amends. She healed a broken relationship by admitting that she was wrong. She died unburdened by her past choices and surrounded by love. If you are ever given a choice between love and anything else, always choose love.

We often think we will have time in the future to forgive and to heal broken relationships, but none of us knows the number of our remaining days. If a chance for forgiveness shows up today, and you are ready and willing, then do it. Forgiveness truly can set you free and bring you peace.

Part of living well means sometimes we need to say we're sorry and ask for forgiveness from friends, family, and even from strangers. And sometimes, we need to pause and remember to forgive that one other person who also deserves to be accepted and unconditionally loved—yourself. We all make mistakes, big or small, after all, and wisdom doesn't come from being a flawless person. Wisdom comes from the steps we take to learn, grow, and heal from our mistakes.

LESSON #6

Forgive yourself, have the courage to admit your own mistakes, and make amends while you still can.

Use the Pink Glitter

So often our everyday lives are focused on tomorrow, causing us to forget about the special moment that we are living in today. It's easy to get lost in our never-ending to-do lists and the hustle and bustle of life, while the days pass us by, one after another. It makes sense how this happens. The future can be an alluring distraction, an invitation to contemplate travel, free time, weight loss and exercise, home improvement projects, or that one new thing you've been meaning to try.

Yes, it's wonderful to have some special occasion to look forward to, but there is another side to our preoccupation with the future that we might want to consider as we move through our life. If we spend too much time thinking about what's to come, and waiting for those distant events, we can easily miss the opportunity to honor the exciting special occasion unfolding right here in the present tense.

One of my clients had candles spread all over her house, in every single room. They were on nightstands and dressers, surrounding her bathtub, and even along the walkway of the woodsy entrance into her house. There were dozens of them, and they were beautiful, but not one of those candles had ever been lit. I imagined how beautiful her home would be in the evenings if she lit those candles, but she told me emphatically that she was saving them for a special gathering, one without a planned date or guest list. She was clinging to the hope for the right time to light the candles. But her time was running out, and so, on one Friday night, she and her partner lit them all, sat quietly in the living room, and enjoyed the flickering flames dancing throughout the house. Her only wish was that she had lit them sooner.

If we live with a mindset that tomorrow is not guaranteed, then indeed, today is a very special day. We would light the candles and drink the good wine.

It took Rosie, a child born with terminal cancer, and her bottle of pink glitter to remind me why it's so important to live each day in the present, as much as we can.

When I met Rosie, she was six years old. She had an indomitable spirit and a spunky personality. I had the great pleasure of spending time with Rosie; her eight-year-old twin brothers, Jackson and Evan; and her nine-year-old sister, Delilah. The kids were energetic, fun-loving, and always up for an adventure. Despite having repeatedly been in and out of the hospital for surgeries and chemotherapy treatments for brain cancer, Rosie was nearly always the liveliest person in the room.

Initially, I was called to offer respite for Rosie's parents, Lyla and Calvin, who were trying to juggle everyday life with small children and two fluffy dogs while also caring for Rosie. They were both physically and emotionally exhausted, tending to Rosie's needs with pure love while also endlessly searching for a new treatment or a clinical trial that might save their daughter's life. Rosie's care took a tremendous amount of time and energy, and her weekly oncology visits usually lasted until late in the afternoon. On those days,

Rosie's parents needed support with the other three children from after school until close to dinnertime.

Every Wednesday, I picked up Rosie's siblings and took them to the park so they could run around and just be kids. We then made our way to their house for a snack, and I helped them with their homework, mostly just making sure it was done. After they got comfortable with me, they began to talk about Rosie and how they were afraid of losing their sister. I was grateful to be there with these children and their sadness. I knew that children's grief often goes unnoticed. They have a way of holding it inside, especially when they know their parents are already filled with their own grief and sadness. Our conversations were so pure, and so hard, but I could sense their need to let their feelings out and talk about it.

This family was full of hope, but they could also feel it slipping away. They longed for the laughter that used to fill the house, and they missed the simple moments around the dinner table sharing "highlights of the day" or answering their favorite question, "What did you do today that was kind?"

Unfortunately, Rosie was getting weaker. She was hospitalized more frequently, her appetite was poor, and she had a hard time sitting for a full meal, so these joyful and "normal" moments became few and far between.

After another month of nonstop treatments, Lyla told me one day that it was time for them to accept the fact that Rosie was going to die. She had just brought Rosie home from yet another extended stay in the hospital. She turned to me and said, "I don't want anyone to ever forget her. I don't want the other kids to forget they had this beautiful sister who loves them so much."

As Lyla cried in my arms, I asked her, "Do you want to work on some art and legacy projects to help the kids remember Rosie?"

Lyla cried even harder and said, "Yes! Yes! I really want to do that. Can we do it soon?"

I immediately found myself working not just with the other children but with Rosie and her parents, too. Together we made a playlist of all of Rosie's favorite songs. We created "The Rosie Jar," a glass jar filled with questions for the family to talk about at the dinner table or when they were gathered in Rosie's room, designed to share memories, and bring the lightness that Lyla craved back into the home. They made finger puppets and told stories about the characters they created. They made concrete stepping stones, embedded with bright plastic jewels, and planted seeds in the garden. Calvin quietly took Rosie's fingerprint to be made into a pendant for Lyla.

Rosie seemed to be steady and pain-free for a couple of months. Almost every visit we painted, at her request. They were a creative bunch, far more creative than me, so I just made sure there were plenty of art supplies and rags to clean up afterward. One day I asked Rosie, "What's your favorite color?"

"Pink glitter!" she said with a giant smile that filled the room. "I love pink glitter! It's so shiny and pretty!"

I asked for a bit more detail, as I had never before seen or heard of the color called pink glitter.

"My mom keeps it on the top shelf, where we can't reach it. It's only for special occasions, like my birthday and sometimes when my best friend, Amanda, comes over."

As Rosie was painting, I asked Lyla about pink glitter. She explained it was a batch of paint that Rosie's grandmother mixed to create a beautiful and shiny pink color. Whenever they used the special pink paint, they sprinkled it with silver glitter on top, and that was how they made the color called pink glitter.

"I don't think we could ever mix that exact color again, so we save it for special occasions," explained Lyla.

I looked at Lyla while trying to form the right words, but I didn't have to. She understood. As she reached up to the top shelf and pulled down the hefty jug of pink glitter, all the children shrieked with delight, none more so than Rosie. After all, it was her favorite color.

We painted with pink glitter for an entire day! Rosie smiled nonstop, and for those short moments, Lyla smiled, too, forgetting about Rosie's bald head and the tumor growing rapidly at the stem of her brain.

The holidays were coming, and Rosie wanted to make something for her family as a surprise. On my next visit, I showed up with new blank canvases and an idea. We divided the canvases in two sections. On the right side of the canvas, each person painted only with their favorite color. On the left side, they painted whatever they wanted.

When I returned a few days later, we dipped Rosie's small hand into a plate of the bright, homemade pink paint, pressed it onto the right side of each painting, and then sprinkled each handprint with loads of silver glitter. They were magnificent. Rosie had created a pink glitter masterpiece for everyone in her family.

Rosie lived comfortably for three more months. She died at home at the age of seven. Weeks later, when I stopped by to visit Rosie's family, the first things I noticed were Rosie's vibrant, pink, and glittery handprint paintings hanging on the wall in the family room.

I will never forget her and the lesson I learned from pink glitter. Rosie did not have the luxury of countless days ahead of her, and we may not either. Instead of waiting for that special day to come, make today a special day and enjoy it fully!

When you look around your house, what are you saving for another day? Can you imagine the joy you might feel right now if you embraced the idea that today is indeed a very special moment? If you had a limited number of days left to live, what would you do differently with those things you've put aside?

Today is a special day, and right now is a special moment.

Rip the tag off that fancy dress and wear it.

If you have fancy bras and underwear, wear them, too.

If you have your favorite chocolate in the refrigerator, eat it.

Open the champagne.

Use the good dishes.

Take a bath with the good bubbles.

Burn the beautiful candle.

Use the pink glitter.

LESSON #7

We don't have to wait for a special moment to celebrate. Find the moment in the present.

Ogres Are Like Onions

I love the movie *Shrek* for an oddly academic reason. Of course, both Shrek and Donkey are completely fascinating and lovable characters, but it is Shrek's one-liner analogy that is near and dear to me. In the movie, while walking through a field of sunflowers, Shrek explains to Donkey that there is a lot more to ogres than people think. He says, "Ogres are like onions, they have layers." I love this because this simple explanation for what Shrek was feeling in the moment also explains my master's research thesis on meaning and purpose in life.

What matters most in life . . . is a lot like an onion. It is often much deeper than what we can easily see, even within our own selves. We need to revisit often what is most important to us, as it changes, it adapts, and it evolves over the course of our lives. This has been confirmed over and over in my work with the dying.

What matters most to you?

It's a short and simple question, yet the answer is never simple. At least not when you begin exploring those inner layers. In our day-to-day lives, we often spend our time and energy on the outer layers and can answer that question without much reflection: What matters most today is that I need to pay the bills, get the kids to school, get some exercise, and meet with my team. The outer layer is us operating on autopilot and what the world sees. While it is meaningful, the outer layer is often covering those vulnerable, tender, deep, and sometimes adventurous layers that make us excited to be alive.

Exploring what matters most is a deeply personal and often challenging journey. It brings purpose and meaning to our lives and is hopefully aligned with our passions. Our priorities about what's most important can stem from an internal longing that tugs at the heart, or it might be an external need for completion or creation of some task or project. Over the course of our lifetimes, the answer to this question will shift and change as we process our thoughts, live our lives, and gain new perspectives.

The beauty and the gift of knowing you're dying is that much of life's superficial and needless tasks quickly fade away. Your to-do list changes drastically. You're forced to fit the remainder of your entire life into the remainder of your numbered days. In my practice, I've seen both great remorse and powerful emotional healing in dying people who were willing to peel away the outer layers to consider what matters most in the time they have remaining.

What matters most to a dying person may sound simple or even mundane to those not facing death, until we remember that each and every ordinary day is a gift.

My client Amanda was a perfect example of this. What was most important to her was to live each day fully, which meant having normal days and spending time with her husband and three teenage children. Each time I visited Amanda, I saw signs of life all around her house. They had two dogs, a few rabbits, and a very active lifestyle. Their house was cluttered with evidence of a busy life . . . dirty dishes, clothes on the floor, and dirt in the form of paw prints dotting the entryway at her front door. It was chaotic with music, loud voices, and laughter. For Amanda and her family, this was their normal.

But one time when I arrived at Amanda's house, something was different. I noticed immediately that there were no paw prints at the front door. Her house was spotless. The kitchen was uncluttered, no clothes on the floors, nothing out of place. Amanda and I sat on the couch and began to talk. The first thing she mentioned was that she had no pain all week, a huge shift from the weeks before. She shared the positive update from her doctor that her tumors had not grown. She told me she had plenty of energy and even attended the final half of each of her kids' sporting events during the week, and then went on a surprise date with her husband. It seemed like Amanda had a wonderful week, so different from the fearful, worried, emotional conversations we had the weeks before. Yet I could tell something wasn't right.

I asked her if anything happened this week that bothered her or that she wanted to talk about. She said, "No, I'm really OK, it was a full week. I'm a little tired, but grateful I got to go out four different times in one week." I commented on how clean her house was this week, and that's when it surfaced.

Her three best friends had come over and cleaned her house so she wouldn't have to worry about doing it herself. They spent almost an entire day cleaning from top to bottom. They organized her drawers, did laundry, and cleaned out the refrigerator. They finished by mopping the paw prints off the entry floor, gave Amanda a big hug, said they would see her again to clean the next week, and left her with a sparkling clean house.

If I were not wearing my doula hat and listening for what wasn't being said, my personal reaction might have been, "Wow, that's so kind of your friends. You must love to have three fairy godmothers come and clean your house for an entire day!" But because I was listening, I could tell that this was where the unspoken words were hiding. I asked her, "What was it like for you to have your friends come in and clean your house?"

Amanda began to cry. "My house doesn't feel like love anymore. It doesn't feel like a family and dogs live here. It doesn't feel like there's a life being lived in the house anymore. I feel so bad for feeling this way, but this clean house makes me so sad and scared. It feels like everyone is getting ready for me to die. I want there to be life in this house today, tomorrow, and every day, even after I'm gone."

Amanda wanted to experience the day-to-day messiness, the noise, and the familiar paw prints on her floor. She wanted to see a large pile of dirty clothes and her kids' fingerprints on the refrigerator door. She wanted to feel alive and see its proof everywhere. She craved everyday life. These may have looked like "outer layers" to her caring friends. But they actually represented the deepest layers of Amanda's meaning and purpose in life, to be enjoyed for the time she had left.

This is a common occurrence when someone is dying. Well-meaning friends and loved ones want to help. They want to lighten the dying person's load, and they often show up in the ways that they themselves would want to be supported in these times. But truly, we are all so different. Some people crave alone time and find it frustrating when there is a constant flow of visitors trying to cheer them up. Most people want to maintain their autonomy and independence as long as possible, so when others step in to "lighten their load," they feel their freedom and their everyday routines slipping away. If you are ever in a position to support someone, don't make assumptions. Simply ask them before doing.

For Amanda, she knew what was meaningful and joyful, and she was living with intention for the time she had left. I suspect that she had lived most of her life this way. Living with the awareness of what is most important in mind can guide you toward an understanding of what areas of your life are flourishing, and what areas might need a little care and nurturing.

When we know what we want and what we need, we can ask for support in ways that serve us best. Amanda spoke with her friends and told them the truth. The next time I showed up at the house, I smiled at the pairs of shoes piled at the front door and the sound of laughter and loud music coming from inside the house. I knew there would be paw prints, fingerprints, and a beautiful mess inside. Amanda left beautiful memories for her husband and kids to treasure . . . and a somewhat messy and well-lived-in house.

In your own precious life, what matters most? Peel away the layers, and don't be afraid of what you find. It will reveal a lot about who you are.

LESSON #8

*Your life doesn't have to look like everyone else's,
so figure out what matters most to you.*

The Many Regrets
of Eleanor Brown

We all have regrets. It's part of being human. The good news is that, if we pay attention, our regrets can be among our greatest teachers.

Think about the last time you said you were going to do something and didn't get around to it. Have you wanted to call someone but didn't have the courage to pick up the phone? Were you unkind to someone but didn't take the time to apologize? Have you wanted to change jobs, travel, start a new hobby, exercise more, quit drinking, take time off, or move to a new town, but life got in the way, and you never got around to it? Regrets come in many forms, and sometimes they are painful to carry, but we can learn a lot about ourselves and make changes in our life if we are willing to acknowledge them as they happen, rather than letting them accumulate.

Don't wait until the end of your life to recognize your goals, dreams, and wishes. Be gentle with yourself for the things you cannot change, and make time to cultivate those things you still can change. At some point, we will all run out of time. There will be no more tomorrows to begin that one thing you have always wanted to do. Instead of enthusiastically saying, "I am going to . . ." you might look back and say with regret, "I really wish I took the time to . . ."

For this reason, I always like to ask my clients if there is anything left undone. This question offers them an opportunity to ponder whether they are ready to let go, or it may reveal whether they are holding on to incomplete tasks that may soon feel urgent to them. It's an opportunity to reflect on any unresolved issues, find peace within, and let go of attachments that may hinder their ability to embrace the end-of-life experience.

When I've asked my clients, "What is left undone?" here are some of their responses:

"I need to write a letter to my children to open after I die. There are so many times I wanted to begin, and I've just kept putting it off. I hope it's not too late." *Frank, age 78*

"I have forgiven everyone who has ever hurt me, teased me, or harmed me in any way. I just wish I could forgive myself, too." *Janelle, age 64*

"My sister told me never to call her again, so I didn't. That was thirty years ago. We haven't spoken since then. Can you help me to call her today? I'm dying and I want to say goodbye." *Benton, age 60*

"My photos, journals, and personal files are a mess. I'd love to tell my family the story of my life. Do you think we have time to organize them?" *Tanya, age 70*

"I have a storage unit and a garage filled to the brim with things my parents and grandparents left for me, which has felt like an insurmountable burden for many years. I need to go through all this stuff so my family doesn't have to."

Ella, age 83

When I posed this question to my client Eleanor Brown, she pulled out a pile of journals she'd been accumulating since her twenty-first birthday. Eleanor was seventy-two and had some exciting adventures in her early years, but the past few decades were marked by inaction and shattered hopes. She told me right from the beginning of our meeting, "My journal entries are sporadic, and there were some good times, but mostly these journals are filled with over fifty years of dreams that never came true."

She was emotional as she flipped through, stopping at some highlighted pages, and reading out loud:

January 3, 1980—This year I'm going back to nursing school. I found an amazing program with enough flexibility so I can work part time, too. I'm so excited!

July 26, 1986—Today Sheila, Beth, and I had a two-hour lunch at the Roadhouse Café. They both have kids now, and Beth is pregnant again. I told them that if Matt and I are ever going to have a family, we need to get started. More sex and a couple of babies sounds like a win/win!

May 9, 1996—This relationship is holding me back. I'm no longer myself and I feel lost. It's time to move on.

April 20, 2000 –My fiftieth birthday came and went. I went into a funk afterward for two full weeks, realizing I'm getting older and still haven't taken the time to follow my dreams. What's wrong with me? I'm so grateful for my wide circle of friends and enjoy all the projects I'm involved in, but I find myself increasingly jealous . . . everyone seems to be having a great time . . . except me. This relationship hasn't gotten any better. I need to move through my fear of being alone. Being alone would be so much better than feeling so unloved.

May 4, 2008—Why am I so scared? I have the freedom to change my life. No one is stopping me. Starting right now, I'm going to be brave and do the things I've always wanted to do.

Eleanor looked up at me with tears streaming down her face. "I didn't do any of these things, not even one of them. Where did the years go? What happened to my life? I guess I always thought there would be more time." We sat together in her sadness, holding space for the grief that came along with her unfulfilled dreams. Her truth was that she waited too long and now it was too late to follow her dreams.

As a death doula, I always do my best to support all my clients in making peace with that bitter reality. A natural inclination would be to try to alleviate someone's sadness, but that isn't my goal. I didn't try to change the subject, point out the good times, or tell Eleanor what I thought she should do. I didn't try to minimize her sadness or take away her pain. I simply listened and acknowledged her feelings. In telling her story, she was able to rest in her sadness and slowly let go. There can be powerful healing when there is a safe space for the truth to be spoken out loud.

I'm glad Eleanor got the chance to talk about her feelings because, the next time I saw her, her attitude had completely changed. She looked radiant and much younger than she did when I saw her two weeks before.

"What have you been up to the past two weeks, Eleanor?" I asked her. "You look like you're filled with energy!"

"I am!" she said enthusiastically. Her fluffy white dog jumped on the bench and cuddled by her side as she continued, "I decided to make lemonade out of all those lemons in my life. I know it's too late for me to travel the world and to find a new love, but it's not too late for me to teach my nieces and nephews so they don't make the same mistakes as me."

Her seven nieces and nephews ranged in age from teenagers to their early twenties. They had come over for a big Sunday brunch in the backyard, and while they were gathered around the table, she told them all about her life. She shared about her early years and the dreams that came true. And then she focused on the long list of ones that never materialized.

She encouraged them to live differently. "Starting today, I want you all to promise me that you will be brave, take chances, and follow your dreams. Don't wait. Do the things that are burning inside you. Pay attention to what breaks your heart wide open. This is where your passion lies. Those will be the things that bring you happiness and success. Someday, you will look back, just like I am now, and when you do, I want you to feel fulfilled . . . I want you to smile through all the decades because you were brave and determined and you tried. That will be a life well lived."

While Eleanor still had a long list of unfulfilled dreams of her own, she was overjoyed to see the hope, passion, and understanding in the eyes of her nieces and nephews. It was clear that she found peace with her past by sharing it with future generations.

Most people still have things they want to do at the end of life. Some have lived fully and intentionally, unafraid to take chances and venture out along the way. Some look back and wish they had. It's easy to imagine which path we'd rather take. I can tell you that Eleanor imagined and dreamed all along the way. She also wished that she had taught her nieces and nephews this lesson by example. It's the choices we make every day that link together to build a life.

Sometimes a client will contemplate what the world will be like when they are no longer here, and they decide there is a little more for them to do. This is when a legacy project becomes important and can bring more meaning, joy, depth, and truth to the dying experience.

You can avoid many regrets and unfinished business by paying attention to what is most important for you to accomplish as you go through your life. Some people like to imagine having only six months to live. It's a good length of time to consider all the areas of their life . . . all the people, the projects, the healing that often comes when time is running out.

If you had only six months to live, what would you do with your sweet, precious time?

Plan for your death, then live your life.

Take that art class.

Learn to speak that language.

Start a nonprofit foundation.

Play that instrument.

Kiss that girl.

Bake that loaf of bread from your grandma's sourdough starter.

Speak in public. Sing in the shower.

Write that poem. Share your story.

Discover what is brewing in your heart and soul. And do that.

Decide to live a life with no unresolved regrets by sharing your heart, following your dreams, and being true to yourself. Live like you have only six months to be alive, and think about what you would do with your time.

LESSON #9

Don't wait. Do the things that tug at your heart, starting today.

Grief Is Love

I thought I understood love. I also thought I understood grief. But then I met my husband, Mark.

Our lives had overlapped over the years through mutual friends and social gatherings. We were casually introduced on several occasions but never had a conversation of any substance. I think that was my fault. Mark was typically with his wife, Ronnie Lew, and instead of taking the time to pause long enough to get to know either of them, I was always rushing through my day. But that didn't stop me from noticing the sweetness between them. It was impossible to miss. Every time I saw them together, they were holding hands in a way that seemed to put everything else in slow motion. I remember feeling a little envious that Ronnie had found someone who was clearly head over heels in love with her.

One day, in my normal rush, I passed them meandering slowly down the center walkway of our local outdoor mall. They were stuck together like glue, laughing, and seemingly enjoying everything about the world around them. As usual, whatever it was that I was doing must have been too important to stop and say hello. Yet for some reason, their joy, their smiles, and that passing moment was seared into my memory. I wondered, "Will I ever know a love like that?"

Mark and Ronnie's life continued to get even better. Before Mark turned forty, he and his business partner sold their successful toy company, offering him and Ronnie the ability to relax, reevaluate their priorities, and simply enjoy life. Mark was living a life that, as a child, he could only dream of. He was happily married and financially secure. He and Ronnie lived in the suburbs with kind and friendly neighbors, traveled, socialized, and had a wonderful life. And there was another exciting life development coming.

Mark and Ronnie both came from good-sized, loving families and dreamed of the same for their life together. Especially for Ronnie, the one piece of life's puzzle that seemed to be missing was children. Finally, after years of trying, they discovered that Ronnie was pregnant . . . not with just one baby, but with triplets! For them, this was the ultimate joy and the beginning of the family they had always wanted. Ronnie looked forward to holding her three babies, and could not wait for Mother's Day, the one day above all others that she always wanted to celebrate.

Early one morning, Ronnie got ready to leave for a meeting, gave Mark a big hug, and told him she would be back right around lunchtime. While at the meeting, Ronnie called Mark to tell him she had a terrible headache and asked if he could please come and pick her up. Mark arrived to see Ronnie, the center of his universe, on a gurney being rushed into an ambulance. Mark turned around and followed the ambulance to the hospital, praying Ronnie would not lose the triplets.

Sadly, it was much worse than he could have ever imagined. Ronnie had had a massive brain aneurysm. After trying everything humanly possible, Mark was devastated to hear that Ronnie had become brain-dead and the triplets could not be saved.

When it was finally time, Mark went into the brightly lit, sterile hospital room to say goodbye to his sweet wife. He leaned in, kissed Ronnie gently, and then in almost a whisper, recited his wedding vows one last time . . . including until death do us part.

Ronnie Lew Button died at 3:05 p.m. on a Sunday afternoon. It was Mother's Day.

Feeling numb and having a sense that life was now in slow motion, Mark walked out of that hospital and into the dark night of grief.

Word of Mark's loss shattered the hearts of all who knew them both. Sympathy cards, books, and flowers filled Mark's home. Mark had the three thousand red roses—Ronnie's favorite—that lined the church during the funeral brought back to their house, where he spent days hanging them upside down from the ceiling of his garage. Grief doesn't always make sense, and this was Mark's way of bringing the outpouring of love for Ronnie back home with him. Still, he was completely broken, feeling like God had ripped him in two, taking the better half and leaving Mark as half a person, helpless and alone.

One day, soon after Ronnie died, I met Mark and his best friend, Dave, for lunch. Dave, who was also a good friend of mine, had jumped in immediately to handle everything for Mark. He rushed to Mark's side at the hospital, contacted friends and family with updates, and reached out to other medical friends and experts to see if the triplets could be saved.

When Dave eventually called me, he was still doing all he could to help. But now, it was more about getting Mark out from under a paralyzing sorrow. Dave was trying to help Mark find a desire to live again. He was worried about Mark being so isolated and empty, so he insisted that Mark go out with friends, just to get out of the house.

At first, I was hesitant to meet the two of them for lunch, not because of his grief and sadness but because I was pregnant and single and didn't want my slightly bulging tummy to upset Mark. After some deep conversations with my best friends, I decided to go and be part of Mark's support system. What started as an awkward and slightly uncomfortable meeting turned into a very raw, very real, very sad, but also very lovely afternoon.

Mark and I began spending more and more time together. I knew his heartache could not be erased, so I didn't even try to take his sadness away. We just sat with it, together . . . me, Mark, and the unwelcome companion named grief. Mark will be the first to admit that he cried on our first twenty dates, and that is not an exaggeration at all, except at the time, we didn't consider them dates. It was more of a blossoming friendship, or perhaps I was a safe place for Mark to rest his broken heart.

Over the next few months, I heard countless stories about Mark and Ronnie, starting with the serendipitous moment they met on a river rafting trip in the Grand Canyon. And every day at 3:05 p.m., Mark's watch would play the familiar ringtone that now memorialized the official moment of Ronnie's death. We would pause and make space for the grief to join us, whatever we were doing.

As our relationship grew deeper, and my stomach grew larger,

Mark and I had a lot to think about. How often does a man lose his wife and babies and then fall in love with a pregnant woman? It was all just too weird. We talked about going our separate ways, but soon realized we would only be doing that for our friends and family who were now worried about both of us and this obviously complicated relationship. We agreed to wait until my baby was born and just observe our own lives unfolding. No one was in a rush anyway.

A few months later, Carly Rose was born in the same hospital, right down the hall from where Ronnie died. In that moment, I cried, as I imagine all new mothers do, with great joy. This new love I felt for Carly was so big, my heart was exploding. And then Mark walked into the hospital room. I watched him as he stared at Carly, taking in every inch of her sweet and perfect face. That was the moment I knew that I would love him forever.

"Say hello to Carly Rose," I said as an invitation for him to come closer.

"She is so beautiful. Both of you are so beautiful," Mark said as he sat by my side. He gave me a gentle hug, and for the first time since I met him, I saw his eyes filled with tears of mostly joy.

Healing takes time and grief can be a lifelong journey, but that day with Mark, I saw a glimmer of hope and felt a shift. I could sense a crack in the door to Mark's heart, an opening with light, love, and life pouring back in.

Before we can ever begin to live with our grief, we must first be willing to step into it.

Let it in.

Be with it.

Let it out.

Repeat.

When we are in deep grief, it can feel like we are carrying a back-pack filled with rocks, weighing us down and keeping us from moving through life with ease. Some grief is heavier than others, but if we don't take the time to feel our grief, it can accumulate over a lifetime and become impossible to carry. But if you take the time to process the smaller losses in life, you will be better prepared when the giant storm of grief that often accompanies the loss of someone you love comes your way.

Allow yourself to feel the loss of your perfect vision when you need reading glasses, or the loss of your ability to run after a knee replacement. Let yourself mourn a breakup, the time you didn't get that promotion you were hoping for, or the time you had to move to a new neighborhood as a young child. It's OK to grieve the loss of your favorite sunglasses or the retirement of your favorite cashier at the corner market. Any loss deserves to be recognized. Grief is our body's natural and very healthy response to loss. By honoring your grief, no matter how big or small, you are honoring a life well-lived and well-loved. We are human, and behind some of our indestructible facades, we all have tender hearts.

One day Mark said, "You know, I've realized lately that I can feel grief and love at the same time, and it actually feels good."

I responded, "Well, maybe grief actually *is* love."

"What do you mean?" Mark asked.

"Part of the reason I love you so much is because of your grief and how you let yourself feel it so deeply. You grieve because you love. Your grief consumed you, but it also showed me how capable you are of deep, deep love. It's sad, but it is also beautiful."

It's been nearly thirty years since Ronnie died. Occasionally Mark will still grieve her death to the point of tears. He looks forward to those moments, and now they bring him great joy.

Like Mark, we must all learn how to honor our grief, along with all the other emotions that make us human. I'd heard the saying "Grief is love with no place to go." That's profound, yet if grief may last a lifetime, then perhaps we need to welcome it and find safe places where our grief can come along for the ride through life with us.

LESSON #10

Do not shy away from grief. It is the clearest and most authentic testament to our love.

Be Kind

Kindness matters. Being kind is an act of generosity that has no downside. A compliment, an act of service, or even simply saying hello to a stranger passing by on the street can benefit someone in ways that we may never even realize. When we are kind to our fellow human beings, we are acknowledging each other and noticing that we all have needs, problems, and struggles in life. Before you are unkind to someone, pause to think about what they might be going through. Chances are, you don't know their story, and showing kindness might lift them up and change their day.

How you treat other people will bring you either peace or despair as you age, and it will certainly affect how you are remembered after you die. What reputation are you building with your words and your actions?

One Saturday afternoon, I attended the funeral of a friendly and outgoing man named Andrew, who was deeply loved and respected in his town. Andrew was only forty years old when he died, just two months after a metastatic pancreatic cancer diagnosis. He left behind both parents, a wife, three siblings, and two teenage children.

Andrew didn't call me because he needed a doula for himself. He called me because he wanted to be sure his wife had someone to talk to about her emotions and fears. I didn't get to know him well, but I promised him I would continue to reach out to his wife, Jenna, so she could talk about her grief and figure out how to go on living without Andrew.

I went to the funeral not only to pay my last respects to Andrew but also to show my support for Jenna and the family. The church was full, as if the entire community showed up to support this beautiful and heartbroken family. The high school choir sang a couple songs and one person after another came to the podium to share stories about Andrew, a beloved high school soccer coach who saw the goodness and potential in everyone.

One man approached the microphone and began crying before he even spoke. "This is hard, standing up here in front of all of you. But I'm here because Andrew has stood up for my family more times than I could ever count." He took a deep breath.

He told the story of his son, Aiden, and how he was constantly bullied at school, even being pushed up against a wall and kicked by one of the bigger kids who always called him names. "Day after day, Aiden was bullied. We tried to put a stop to it, and sometimes it would be calm for a few weeks, but then it would start up again. The only reason Aiden was able to keep going to school was because of Coach Andrew. Every day, Aiden went to soccer practice after school, and every day, Coach Andrew would build him back up . . . every single day."

He paused for another deep breath and to wipe his eyes before he continued, "I know Andrew talked to the bullies, but it was how he treated Aiden that meant so much to me. Andrew would tell Aiden, 'I see you. I believe in you. And you matter. Don't you ever forget it.' Andrew gave Aiden confidence, strength, and courage. He has slowly learned to stand up for himself. He speaks up, and he looks out for other kids now, too. And I have Coach Andrew to thank for that."

He looked over at Jenna and said, "Your husband was a good man."

Stories of Andrew's kindness brought tears to my eyes, and I felt inspired by his connection to so many people. I left the church, and was just a few steps from the crosswalk, when I noticed Andrew's parents walking ahead of me. Andrew's mom was crying. His dad tenderly held her arm, whispered something in her ear, and helped her stay steady as they stepped into the crosswalk just as the light had changed.

Suddenly, a car came speeding down the road right toward them. The driver slammed on the brakes and came to a halt. He rolled down his window and yelled to Andrew's dad, "Are you a fucking moron?" And then he raised his hand up in disgust, mumbled something else, and drove away.

I wanted to run after that man and say, "This man's son just died. These sweet people are grieving. They are leaving a funeral and heading to the cemetery down the road to bury their son. Be kind. You don't know their story."

All I could do was rush ahead, gently take Andrew's mom's other arm, and help them across the street and into their car. They were distraught, and maybe this rude man who yelled at them didn't even faze them, as their grief was already so, so deep. But I felt sad for

Andrew's parents. I couldn't help myself. I drove home wondering if that man would ever stop to think about how unkind he was to those two people on such a sad day. I hope so.

People who live their lives with a pattern of treating others with such abruptness and disregard are often filled with regrets toward the end of their lives. Some are hard to hear and take a lot to process, but most are everyday poor choices, like yelling at a grieving couple, that we have made along the way. I've had clients in their eighties feeling remorse for making a judgmental comment to a mother struggling trying to soothe her crying baby, or for being rude to a bank teller four decades ago. Others have lost opportunities, lost their moral compass, or, like my client Bo, caused harm to others and lost relationships.

Bo was a sixty-one-year-old man with Parkinson's disease. He lived alone for two decades until he needed extra care and moved back to the town where his kids and ex-wife still lived. Bo moved in with his youngest daughter, Joon, whose husband was in the army and deployed at the time. This was a good thing for Bo, because he had certain expectations for his daughter and never welcomed Joon's husband into his life, or his home.

It was a struggle for Bo to be away from his familiar environment and to be dependent on others. The first day at Joon's house he lamented, "I've spent my entire life not needing anyone. I really don't want to start now." But within days, he let his walls down and let the care in. The family treated him with tender love and respect. His children, grandchildren, and even his ex-wife rotated shifts to care for him in what turned out to be the final weeks of his life.

One day, Joon talked to Bo and me about her husband, Jack. She was so proud of his service to our country and grateful he was deployed to Italy, a relatively safe place considering all the unrest in the world.

"Dad, I know you've never liked Jack, but he wanted me to tell you he's been thinking about you. He told me to say thank you, from him to you, for bringing such a beautiful woman into the world for him to love," Joon said sweetly.

Bo looked away from Joon. His eyes filled with tears. "I'm sorry, Joon. I wanted you to marry someone else, and that was wrong. I haven't been kind to Jack, and I'm so, so sorry. He's been good to you, given me two wonderful grandchildren, and given you a beautiful life. I look around this house, and I see how loved you are. He must be a special man."

"Thank you, Dad. That means so much to me," said Joon. "I wish you would've gotten to know him. He's a really special man, and an amazing father."

And that was it. Days passed and it felt like healing was happening in the house . . . slow, sweet, and meaningful healing. Joon needed to hear Bo acknowledge that he had been unkind and appreciated her dad for his willingness to apologize. Bo had missed out on years of precious time with his daughter and his grandkids because of his selfish opinions and harsh words that pushed Joon and Jack away years ago, and that was a regret he needed to say out loud. He could not change his past, but he was given a gift, a second chance to change the rest of his story.

Early one Saturday morning, Joon called me. "My dad was restless all night long. He keeps saying he's ready to get on a plane, but he can't get there yet. I don't know what he's talking about. Can you come over for a while?"

I assured Joon I'd come by and that this was not unusual. Many people reference trips and travel before they die.

Bo greeted me by name and reached his arm out to the chair by his side, inviting me to sit down. He seemed lucid and aware. Joon sat on the other side of the bed.

"How are you feeling right now?" I asked Bo.

"I feel like I'm going to die soon, and I'm not ready," he replied.

"Do you know what might be holding you back?" I asked.

"No, not really," Bo said, shaking his head.

Joon interrupted, "Dad said he was about to go to the airport to catch a plane, but that he wasn't ready just yet."

I was hoping to get Bo talking about the trip, thinking it might be linked to his hesitation about dying, so I asked him a question that just felt right at the time. "Bo, where were you going on that plane?"

"I was going to fly around the world to see old friends to say goodbye. And I was going to Italy."

"Italy?" I paused and looked at him. "Were you going to see Jack?"

A tear dropped from Bo's eye. "Yes. I think I was."

I looked over at Joon and saw the tears streaming down her face.

Thankfully it was early evening in Italy, and Joon was able to reach Jack. She explained the situation to him, and soon Jack was on the phone, video chatting with Bo.

Bo spoke from his heart. His voice was weak, but his words were strong. "I'm so sorry, Jack. I've treated you poorly because of my own selfish wishes, and I was wrong. You've been so good to Joon and all my family. I know you are a good man. I'm so sorry, Jack. Will you forgive me?"

"Yes, sir. I forgive you. And I promise to take care of Joon and your family for the rest of my life. Thank you for calling, sir. This means a lot to me."

"Thank you," Bo whispered.

Bo was able to say the words he had been holding inside, releasing the emotional burden that was keeping him tethered to this life. A couple hours later, Bo fell asleep. Joon heard him talking about getting on the plane again, but this time he made it. Joon held his hand as he took his final breath. Now he was free.

We all have the choice to be kind. A compassionate heart leads to a life well lived.

LESSON #11

Be kind. You will remember when you weren't.

I Love You, Too

It's been said that, in addition to gravity and momentum, it's really love that makes the world go round. In my experience, it is also the topic of some of the most frequently asked questions at the end of life:

Did I love well?

Was I loved?

Do the people I love know that I love them?

Love is complicated. It includes so many of our relationships, including our birth families, our chosen families, friendships, romantic partners, people we know for certain seasons of our lives, and random acquaintances we meet along the journey of our life. But when you get to the end of your life, you will most likely want to be with the people who have been by your side through the ups and downs and the ones who mean the most to you. There is peace and comfort in being surrounded by those very special people. After someone dies, often the only thing left in the room is love.

This is why I always ask my clients, "Who matters most to you?" Part of it is getting to know their support system and who will be caring for them. Part of it is about healing broken relationships, apologizing, forgiving each other, and sharing our hearts. But most of all, I want to know whom they want to surround them at the bedside when they take their final breath.

When I ask my clients who matters most, they share from their hearts:

> "My parents. I feel sad they are losing a child. I can't imagine that, but I want them to know they made me the person I am today."
>
> *Jenny, age 52*

> "I hope that my three kids, their children, and the great-grandchildren will be gathered around my bed so I can hear their voices one last time."
>
> *Zhang, age 87*

> "There are so many people who have been there for me. When I scan all the years, there were teachers, neighbors, my best friend's parents, our youth pastor, and the guy who took a chance and hired me when I really needed a job. My life would have been so different without them. Some of them will never know how they changed my life."
>
> *Dwayne, age 70*

> "This may sound weird, but as death draws near, I'm dreaming about my ancestors and those who I hope are there to greet me as I leave this life for whatever is to come next . . . the great unknown. I miss those people who loved me so much."
>
> *Marilyn, age 96*

Have you ever thought about who you might want to see if it were your last week of life? Or whose hand you would want to hold as you take your final breath? These are your people, the ones you love and the ones who love you back.

Some of us love others well, but we aren't so great about letting ourselves be loved in return, especially if we've been hurt in the past. Maybe this is how we protected ourselves. Letting yourself be loved is a choice. It took me more than a couple of decades to realize this, so I share this with grace for those of you who still guard your hearts. But when you are ready, and have the opportunity, let love in. It feels good to have a safe and supportive person loving you and cheering you on through the good times and the hard times.

My doula partner, Sarah Hill, can tell you a lot about being loved. Her own mom died when she was just four years old, yet Sarah recalls with great fondness that she was loved deeply. "We loved one another so thoroughly in those first few years of my life that our bond is forged in forever."

Sarah is the type of person who builds deep and lasting relationships within the doula community, with her clients, and in her own personal life. She credits her mom for planting the seeds of her doula heart and giving her the ability to say "I love you" freely and wholeheartedly. She means it. And when her clients grieve, she grieves with them.

When Sarah was just four years old, her attachment to her mom made an imprint on her heart and taught her to love and to also be loved. As much as Sarah and I are alike, in this way we are very different. Sarah wears her heart on her sleeve. I tended to keep mine neatly and safely tucked away, only to make an appearance after much time and consideration. As a child, I was not accustomed to receiving outward expressions of love, so I had to learn to trust and let my guard down. And now, as the decades have passed, I see that the walls of protection around my heart may have kept some bad experiences out, but those same walls have kept some love out, too. After years of deep personal work, I have changed. My family can feel my love, and though I am not one to greet my friends with kisses and excessive gushing, they know I love them, too.

But what about everyone else? Do they know how I feel about them? What about all the clients I have been with on their death-beds? What about mentors, teachers, the village of people who helped raise my kids, the doctors and nurses who cared for me during my journey with breast cancer? Or our small-town country doctor who would stitch my active, surf-loving husband's head or foot at least once a year on a Saturday when his office was closed? I will never forget his kindness and care.

These people all loved my family and me so well, and after seeing how Sarah shares her heart so freely, I wondered if I ever truly let them know how much I love them all. And one thing I know for sure, even if I do put my love and care out into the world, sometimes I still have a hard time letting love in.

Even though I may not have said it out loud, I believe my clients all knew I cared deeply for them, in my own slightly reserved way. I always tend to my clients' needs and wishes with reverence, respect, and love. They can count on me to show up and to accept them in whatever state they are in that day. They know I care, even though I may not pause to say "I love you" or express my feelings for them. And maybe that is OK. Maybe it's good enough that they just simply know by my actions. But Sarah got me thinking, especially after we spent an evening together with our client Joni.

When we first received the call about Joni, we were told by the palliative care doctor that she was living in a difficult situation and that she needed to move immediately. The friend who had taken her in was becoming uncomfortable with Joni's increasing medical needs, home hospice visits, and the supplies that were piling up inside the small, shared living space. Joni told us her friend asked her to leave because she didn't want her "to get sicker and die" in her home. Joni was in relentless pain from the ovarian cancer that was taking over her body. She was alone, penniless, and scared, and she needed some support.

We were also informed that Joni had been approved for medical aid in dying (MAID), which means she could take medications to end her life and avoid the intractable pain and suffering that made her life miserable. MAID originated in Oregon in 1997 and is becoming more widely available as new laws are passed each year. Joni met all the criteria, including having a terminal diagnosis with six months or less to live, the mental capacity to make this decision on her own, and the physical ability to take the medications herself.

That evening, Sarah called Joni. Intending it to be a quick introductory call, Sarah slipped downstairs into a small, private space where she could introduce herself to Joni. She planned to set up an appointment, let Joni know the two of us would be her doulas, and then run back upstairs to put her son to bed. Thankfully, Sarah's husband took care of the bedtime stories that night, because over two hours passed with Sarah huddled in that small space talking to Joni. Sarah heard about Joni's life, the rags-to-riches story, and then the riches-back-to-rags-again story. She heard about the relationships along the way, including the one that brought her to that night, talking to Sarah on the phone from a tiny, cold bedroom and an unwelcoming situation.

Not only was Joni in constant pain but there was an excruciating, burning sensation that had taken the joy out of her once beautiful life. The cancer had spread to her liver and lungs. Her chest felt tight, her breathing was labored most of the time, and she was often doubled over and crying from the sharp stabbing pains in her abdomen. Every day was worse than the day before. While she loved her life, Joni knew that she would never live another day without terrible pain and suffering. She was planning to take the MAID medications soon, but she needed a place to die.

The next day, Sarah and the hospice social worker got together and soon had a plan in place for Joni. Miraculously, and because it was the end of the month, they found an empty bed in a residential care home. Joni packed up her meager belongings and went to spend her final nights there.

Over those next few days, Sarah and Joni became like familiar, close friends, because that's what Sarah does. She loves, and she lets herself be loved. I felt connected to Joni as well. Sarah was the lead doula, so she had the ongoing contact with Joni, but the three of us were communicating via email and through Sarah, so I felt a warm, playful, and wise energy from Joni and was looking forward to meeting her.

Our work can be so peculiar at times like these. To meet someone and connect with them immediately, knowing that they will die very soon, brings up indescribable emotions. As Sarah and I drove to be with Joni when she took her final medications, Sarah began telling me the stories Joni shared with her during their lengthy phone calls.

Sarah began, "I'm really looking forward to meeting Joni. I know we're going to love her. She was a powerful woman, and she still is. Her sense of self and her intentional way of living and caring for others is truly beautiful. She's had a great life, not without tragedy, but she was always grateful, joyful, and energetic, and lived life with gusto and a sense of divine purpose. She feels her higher power guiding her and has no spiritual discomfort at all. She said she's fully at peace. While some of her relationships are in disrepair, she feels at peace with those, too. Her boundaries are solid, and she feels like she has healed everything that can be healed in her precious lifetime. She is ready to die."

We pulled up to the residential care home and parked.

The room was stark and simple, but Joni's warm, genuine smile filled the room with beauty and light. In the corner was a small suitcase she brought to the care home holding what remained of her once full life. Her toiletries sat on the side table in a small ziplock bag. Her robe and a light blanket were folded neatly side by side on the dresser. There were a couple of colorful dresses hanging in the closet and some folders at the foot of her bed.

She reached out her arms and took our hands, sincerely happy to meet us on what would be the last night of her life. She wanted to talk about us, our families, our work, and what we do for fun. Once we finished talking, Joni told us she was ready. We settled in and made sure she was comfortable. She instructed us to wash her face and hands and to dress her after she died in one of the two dresses hanging in the closet. She wanted us to choose which dress we liked best. Coincidentally, we brought flowers that night, and the oranges and purples matched perfectly with one of the bright, floral dresses in the closet.

Sarah and I gathered by Joni's bedside. "I'm ready. Is there anything else we need to do?" Joni asked, looking back and forth at Sarah and me.

"No, we just want you to be comfortable. Is there anything else you feel you need or want to do, or anything you want to talk about?" we asked her.

"Well, yes, there is just one thing." Sarah and I paused as Joni took our hands and looked deeply into each of our eyes. "I just want you two to know that both of you are beautiful. You are kind, compassionate, and your eyes are shining . . . both of you have eyes that are so gentle. I'm so glad you both are here to spend this time with me. I love you."

I was stunned.

Sarah leaned forward and said, "I love you, too, Joni."

I held Joni's hand a little tighter and probably stuttered a bit, but I said, "I love you, too, Joni." And I meant it. I loved her. She was pure, genuine, kind, joyful, graceful, beautiful, authentic, and fully engaged and present. What an amazing woman she was. Her last words were expressions of love for two people she had just met.

After she died, we washed Joni's body gently, put on her bright, multicolored dress, and brushed her strawberry blonde hair. We laid the flowers on her chest and wrapped her hands around the stems. We could hear the crickets chirping outside as the night air blew through the room. She was at peace.

Joni knew how to be loved and how to love others without judgment or expectation. She had a pure and uncomplicated love for humanity, which was so inspiring. I am forever grateful that, on that night, she wrapped Sarah and me into her heart.

Joni taught me that love comes easy with an open heart. She let love flow freely through her and always shared her love by telling people how they made her feel, up until her very last breath.

LESSON #12

*Make a conscious effort to freely
speak your love for others.*

The Hard Stuff

After nearly two decades of working in end-of-life care, I am still in awe of the cycle of life, and the fact that every single one of us ends each day a little bit closer to our final day. Yet, none of us knows when it will be our turn. It is an unknown that we live with every day, even though we may not think about it. And, because we don't do a great job of talking openly about it, when we are finally facing death, it often hits us by surprise. We live each day as if the rules don't apply to us, as if any of us might just be that one bizarre anomaly in the universe, the one and only person who will actually *not* die. And then, one day, we realize that is not going to be the case.

I used to question my decision to do this work. After all, what do I know about dying? Yes, I've had loved ones die, and I had breast cancer that had me wondering for many months if I would live or die, but to actually understand what someone is experiencing while letting go of this wild and beautiful life is something else altogether.

However, along the way, I learned that indeed I can do this work. So often we tell ourselves that something is too challenging, too difficult, too hard, or too emotional, and we talk ourselves out of even trying. In most cases, this is simply not true. We humans can do challenging, difficult, hard, and emotional things. We do them all the time, sometimes without even realizing it. No experiences are exactly the same, so in truth, we are always learning and being exposed to new moments. Before you take on something that seems out of your reach, it's helpful to remember that an open mind and an awareness that you don't always have to know the answers will give you the courage to show up and do those hard and difficult things in life.

Hospice chaplain Clarence Liu was my mentor. He was gentle, wise, and unflappable. When I first met him, I was new to doula work, so I watched his every move. I paid close attention to his calm and centered body language and listened to every thoughtful word he shared with his patients. He was naturally adept at knowing what to say and do, and I wondered if I would ever get to a place where I would feel as comfortable stepping into the home of a dying person with such ease and grace.

One very memorable day, we were driving to visit Matt, a man dying of cancer who was struggling with some fears around the afterlife and his beliefs. Clarence told me he wanted me to be part of the conversation, too, and that we would work together to support Matt in whatever way we could. I was petrified, but also determined to learn from Clarence, who seemed so comfortable driving to Matt's house without concern about what was to come. I was feeling anxious, so I unloaded all my thoughts and questions before we arrived.

"Clarence, how do you do this? How will I know what to say? How will I know what to do? What about all the other people in the room? Do we talk to them all, do we let them speak first, how do we start the conversation?"

My mind filled with questions, but Clarence taught me right away that I was approaching it all wrong. He suggested I learn a bit about the Zen Buddhist concept of "beginner's mind" to see if that might guide me to be more comfortable with the uncertainty of this work.

Then, just before we got out of the car, with Clarence probably sensing my nerves, he gave me a little hint.

"Diane, have you had a conversation with someone with cancer before?"

"Yes, I have," I replied.

"But have you had a conversation with *this* person with cancer before?"

"No," I answered.

"Have you seen someone die before?" he asked me.

"Yes, I have," I replied.

"But have you seen *this* person die before?" Clarence asked, looking into my eyes.

"No," I replied, starting to understand.

"Then this is all new. Let it be new. Bring your heart, your curiosity, and your open mind. Leave the rest behind," Clarence said as he shut the car door and began walking toward Matt's house.

That evening, I started learning about beginner's mind, a practice of setting aside your preconceived notions of what to expect and seeing the world through fresh eyes. It struck me immediately that there is freedom in not feeling like I need to always know exactly what to say or do, or how to solve a problem.

Imagine giving yourself permission to say "I don't know" and to feel good about it! None of us are experts, and the sooner we accept that, the sooner we can stop trying to control life and impress others. Over the years, the concept of beginner's mind has become a core foundation for my doula work as well as for my everyday life. It keeps us humble, and curious.

It was refreshing to realize that I didn't need to know the answers to everything I was asked. In fact, cultivating a beginner's mind meant that I could see my clients with fresh eyes at every visit. I no longer knocked on the door with an agenda or an opinion. I simply showed up and allowed space for whatever happened that day. My work became so much easier, and I felt free, present, openhearted, and more accepting.

Clarence Liu taught me how to be still, how to be present, and how to show up fully for whatever situation came our way. I asked him one day, "Clarence, have you always been this peaceful and calm?"

He actually laughed. "Oh, no. You wouldn't believe how scared I was when I first started out. Did I ever tell you about one of the very first cases I had as a new chaplain?"

Clarence had been a chaplain for only about three months when he was contacted by a funeral home director with a request. He was asked to sit with a couple who had just lost their one-year-old baby. They were coming for a viewing the next day, and the funeral director thought the bereaved couple would appreciate the support.

This unexpected request made Clarence uncomfortable, but he said, "Of course I'll be there."

Clarence lay in bed that night, worried about and wondering what to say to this couple whose lives had been suddenly shattered.

He arrived early, giving himself time to meet the funeral director and to settle into the reality of what was about to happen. He found himself feeling nervous, unqualified, and ill-equipped to be with this level of deep grief.

He looked at the funeral director, who likely sensed his insecurity, and said, "I think I need to sit with the baby first." Somehow, Clarence just knew it was something he needed to do.

Clarence was escorted into a room that felt way too large for such a teeny-tiny bassinet. Lying there on a table surrounded by flowers was a beautiful baby girl wrapped in a soft blanket. Clarence recalled that the room was filled with sadness, yet also with peace. He wasn't quite sure how to feel, so he sat, honoring his lack of familiarity. Beginner's mind, he reflected. He sat in stillness, looking at this sweet baby.

Suddenly he felt himself tearing up. He noticed it, and normally might have tried to hold it together, but he decided to let the feelings come out. Within seconds, he found himself sobbing uncontrollably, alone with the baby, contemplating life and loss and love and grief and all the emotions we experience over the course of our lives. The voice in his head told him to breathe, just sit there, and let the tears flow.

So, he did.

Once he stopped fighting his emotions and let them out, he felt less anxious and worried. He had become good at controlling his tears, and his emotions, but not this day. He sat quietly while more tears starting flowing. He continued telling himself, "Just be. Just be still. It's OK. Let it out."

Clarence quickly gathered himself together as he heard talking outside the door. He greeted the parents and walked them into the room to be with their daughter one last time. They wailed, and then they stopped and shared memories.

Then they cried some more, and the mom asked, "Can I hold her?"

"Yes, of course you can hold her. She's your daughter." Clarence's soft voice was filled with compassion for the heartbreak he was witnessing.

She cradled the baby in her arms and rocked her, singing the songs she had hoped to sing to her sweet baby for years to come. And then they cried again, and again, and again, until the tears became soft and quiet.

Clarence knew there were no words to say. There was nothing he could fix. He had learned how to just sit, and not react. And he had learned earlier that day to let all the emotions in the room flow freely. So, once again, he made space for the unimaginable grief, and also for the abundant love.

There was noise outside the door. Clarence hadn't expected both sets of grandparents and some siblings, but there they were. The mom continued to hold her baby, and soon the entire room was filled again with tears and tremendous grief, and then some shared memories, and then more tears, and some songs, and more tears, and poems, and even some sweet laughter, and then more tears.

The child's father asked Clarence to pray. Unprepared, but fully present, Clarence allowed the voice of God to speak through him. The family sensed the heartfelt love and the power of Clarence's words that filled the room. Big words, spoken in a small, soft voice, respecting the moment. More tears, a few more stories, and then a tender and heart-wrenching final goodbye.

Clarence had spent the entire night before lying awake in bed worrying about what to say to this grieving family, but he showed up with beginner's mind and a warm heart. He didn't need to plan out what words he would say. He simply needed to trust that the words would come.

Clarence knew that giving himself permission to feel his deepest feelings was the way to live in full integrity and truth, but this was the first time in a long time that he had let his emotions be free in a way that was spontaneous, pure, and authentic. He learned how to grieve that day, and that it's OK to hurt and to mourn. He learned that we must be in our hearts to do this work, and sometimes our hearts get broken open. He learned that growth happens in the hard stuff. And he remembered that, by practicing beginner's mind and leaving his expectations at the door, he could do hard and difficult things. We all can.

Life is not always easy and there are always going to be challenges, but don't let that stop you from living a full and meaningful life.

Trust your heart and your mind.

Trust that you can do hard things.

LESSON #13

You don't have to have all the answers.
Just show up with an open heart and mind.

Jesus Makes Casseroles

Big changes can happen when one person is willing to take small steps to make life better for people, animals, or our planet in any way that calls to them. Not only will others benefit when you make a difference in the lives of others, but a generous heart is rewarded in ways that you may not even notice. The saying "It's better to give than to receive" is true for many reasons. A kind gesture or words of encouragement can change someone's life, but it can change your life, too. A practice of generosity can bring you increased happiness, less stress, and a greater sense of overall well-being. Being generous brings us joy and satisfaction, helps us to see beyond our own personal story, and fosters a sense of compassion for the struggles and suffering of others.

For most of us, giving and generosity will focus on a personal component that has little to do with money or saving the world. It's about small acts of kindness. It's about taking out the trash on Monday morning for the older gentleman who lives next door. It's about the compassionate hairdresser who offers free haircuts to the unhoused people in her community the first Tuesday of every month. It's about a child sharing their lunch with a friend who forgot theirs or the customer service person who takes the time to listen to a stranger's story. And I know from many of my clients, as well as my own personal experience with breast cancer, there are many angels among us who are willing to deliver meals with love to the sick and the hurting.

Over the years I've learned that you will most likely feel good about your life and its purpose if you are generous with your time. If you can build a hospital wing or cure a disease, absolutely, that's a wonderful and important achievement. However, loving each other well, one person at a time, makes the world go round in a hopeful and meaningful way. If you learn to serve others in your everyday life, in everyday ways, it will be easier for you to answer some of the most important questions that people consider toward the end of life:

Did my life matter?

Did I make a difference?

Is the world a better place because I was here?

When it comes to giving and generosity, the small things are also the big things. Think about how good you feel when someone holds a door open for you, returns your lost wallet, or lets you go ahead in line when you have only a couple of items in your cart. These are all meaningful gestures of generosity.

When I was first diagnosed with breast cancer, our family had been living in Nashville, Tennessee, for only about a year. Whether it was divine providence or sheer luck, during a time when our family truly needed help, people showed up from almost everywhere.

One day, my neighbor Becky stopped over to check on me. After giving me a huge hug, she informed me in no uncertain terms that I would not be cooking or worrying about dinner for the next few months. She explained that this is what Nashville women do for each other, especially when it's a mom with young kids. I stood there, speechless, with tears rolling down my face as she turned around and walked out without giving me a chance to say a word.

Within days, I was presented with a calendar for the entire month of November, with a list of the families who signed up to bring us food while I was recovering from surgery and starting chemotherapy treatments. I stared at the calendar and cried again in gratitude for each and every name on that page. I think I cried even a little harder for the names of the generous people on that list I didn't recognize, those giant-hearted humans I had never met before.

Four nights a week, the doorbell rang, and a new meal would arrive for my family and me. The food just kept coming, and my young kids loved it! They were constantly writing thank-you notes and stopping moms in the hallways at school to thank them for their meals.

I never realized how many variations on casseroles there are or how delicious they can be until this experience. We had casseroles made of veggies, meat, rice, or noodles, casseroles as a main dish or as a side, breakfast casseroles, and dessert casseroles. If you can casserole it, my family has probably had it. I completely understand why it's the perfect food to bring to a family for dinner. It heats up easily and always lasts for two meals. I lost count at about forty-two casseroles, and we loved them all.

One night during dinner, my husband, Mark, said, "I think Jesus is a very busy woman who makes casseroles."

Looking back, I think the hard times were really some of the best times. I felt love in every casserole I received and every casserole I have witnessed since then. Casseroles are not small things, and I still wonder if there really are small things. From what I have seen, all acts of generosity are giant, loving hugs.

I see generosity of spirit as a key factor in creating peace and expressing love for those who are sick and dying. But even in our everyday life, and even when we are healthy and strong, we need each other. We always have. We always will.

At sixty years old, my client Martine inspired me because his creativity and his passion for others seemed to be the perfect elixir for his pain and suffering. When I met him, he had just started his third round of treatments for an aggressive cancer, but he was determined to go on living a full life for as long as he could. Martine lived with three of his six children, their partners, and all their children. He was always surrounded by a lot of love.

When I first began visiting Martine, he didn't strike me as someone who was dying anytime soon. I was told by his children that he was still working to the point of exhaustion, came home late from work most days, and then played with his grandkids before falling asleep on the sofa each night. His sons and daughter were worried about him staying so busy, especially after the doctor told him to take it easy and get some rest.

During my second conversation with Martine, I learned he was a respected local contractor and that he wasn't really staying late to work at his job every evening. Instead, he was leaving work and going to build a fence for a young, single mom who needed a safe place for her kids to play. I also learned that, before starting the fence project, he rebuilt the kitchen in another family's home, just to help them out. He showed me the picture with great pride and personal satisfaction, not because he did something wonderful, but because he had learned so many skills in his lifetime and was understandably quite proud of his work. I could see from his own apartment how skilled he was. His workmanship was lovely, but it was his heartfelt desire to serve others that I found most inspiring.

One day, after his kids nudged me to talk to him about slowing down, I said, "Martine, you've been working six days a week ever since we first met. Are you feeling like you're getting enough rest and sleep?"

He told me point-blank, "The best part of my life, aside from my family, is to be able to help others. I'm not going to stop caring for my neighbors until my feet cannot walk and my arms cannot hug."

When we give, share, and care for others, it makes others feel good, but it makes us feel good, too. There are many ways to be generous, including sharing your time, talents, energy, and words. It is a lifestyle choice to live in ways that benefit others. If you serve others over and over again, it becomes a habit and a way of life. Martine was dying of cancer, but caring for others in his community was still a priority for him. He understood the value, both for the giver and the receiver, and he didn't want to let go of that uplifting part of his life.

I remember one of the last days I saw Martine alive. As I walked toward his apartment, I noticed people laughing, music playing, and kids running around. I could smell the home-cooked food from the place next door. There were signs of a bustling life all around me.

But when I got to Martine's door, it was silent. I knocked gently, and when I opened the door, I saw the family circled around him, holding rosary beads, heads bowed, and praying.

He had fallen the day before, and he was resting. He was unable to walk, so the family brought his bed into the living room, where they could all be huddled together. Everyone was calm, and the only thing I could feel in the room was warmth and love.

While we were talking, the doorbell rang. Martine's son opened the door, and a young couple and two kids entered and walked directly toward the kitchen in a straight line. The woman greeted everyone but continued walking past us, holding a large platter of food, covered with foil and towels to keep it warm. Her husband carried a clear plastic bowl overflowing with lettuce and tomatoes. Their daughter followed with a large bag of tangerines, and the little boy, who was about five years old, was swinging a bag of tortillas by his side.

"This smells so good, Elena! You are such a fantastic cook! I can't wait to eat! This looks delicious!" Martine's family were all enthusiastically thanking Elena and applauding her wonderful cooking skills and the savory aroma that drew them all into the kitchen.

"What's for dinner, Elena?" asked one of the grandkids.

"It's pastel azteca. Your grandfather's favorite dish!" said Elena proudly.

She looked over at me, and I said, "It smells so delicious, Elena. What's pastel azteca?"

"It's like a Mexican casserole," she said with a smile.

I smiled back, not only to acknowledge her smile but also because, in that moment, I saw Jesus again.

And in that moment, Jesus was a four-feet-ten lady with a loving, generous heart and a fresh-baked casserole.

While we were chatting, the little boy opened the bag of tangerines. He took one out and walked over to Martine, who was resting with his eyes closed. The boy gently opened Martine's hand and set a tangerine in his palm.

A homemade casserole or even one small tangerine, offered with love, can bring so much comfort and light to those who are suffering or lonely. But you don't need to make casseroles. Even a handshake or a hug can make someone's day. Be that person.

Be generous with your hands and your heart. No matter who you are, you're never too young, or too old, to make a difference.

LESSON #14

*The world is a better place when we
serve others in everyday ways.*

Time Only Goes

We live as if we can control the hands of time.

We spend time, waste time, lose time, save time, kill time, and buy time. We live as if the clock ticks based on our own needs and desires. But the truth is, time is our most treasured resource. Not only is it finite and non-renewable but we never know how much of it we have.

Many of my clients lament the countless hours they spent working and the family gatherings and celebrations they missed. They talk about hours spent working "so I can get two weeks off a year" rather than working for something they believe in, something that is satisfying, or something that allows them to create and enjoy the life they want.

One client was given a pair of tall plastic rain boots as a retirement gift, after working as a contractor for thirty years. "That was it," he said. "A pair of plastic rain boots."

He left work on his last day feeling like his bosses didn't even consider the heart he had put into his job, or all the time he committed along the way. He said, "If these boots could talk, they would tell the story of the thousands and thousands of hours I've worked in the pouring rain. They may tell you where I've been all those years, but they say nothing about who I am. It feels like I wasted so much time at my job."

Another client, Inga, told me she spent two decades working at a marketing company, only to be told at the age of forty-eight that "she no longer had the right vibe for the position" and was let go. Just like that. Loyalty was a one-way street, and she was left resenting the time she had invested so that others could shine and get promoted. What Inga regretted the most about working so hard was the moments she missed in her children's lives, moments she could never get back.

A very memorable client taught me a lot about how we spend our time. I share this story because it applies to so many of us . . . maybe not the money . . . but the message.

Hendricks was a seventy-year-old man dying from coronary heart disease. He already had two cardiac bypass surgeries and a pacemaker. During his last surgery, he had another heart attack. The doctors told him he needed to eliminate stress, increase his exercise, and change his diet completely if he wanted to live another year. This was challenging for Hendricks, who loved working and wasn't ready to slow down. He wanted to talk to me about his future, but it turned out that we spent most of our time together talking about the past.

When I first pulled up to Hendricks's home, I was greeted by an enormous gate. I'd never seen such an elaborate entrance to a private home before. I laughed to myself, thinking I would need an annual pass or to pay a fee to enter. I punched in the code, and the double doors opened to reveal a giant mansion sitting at the top of the long driveway, lined on both sides with grapevines that went on as far as my eyes could see.

I gasped out loud as a thought filled my mind: "Hendricks lives here . . . alone."

After a few weeks of working together, I arrived one day and saw him outside, just beyond the tall glass sliding doors in the living room. He was sitting on the porch in a rocking chair overlooking the endless vineyard below. He was expecting me and placed a glass of water on the table. A light blanket was waiting for me on the small couch next to him.

He was a quiet man, but over time I realized that his words were chosen carefully and only spoken after much introspection. He didn't say hello that day. Instead, he stayed with his thoughts until he abruptly said, "I've been obsessed with grapes my entire life."

After a deep sigh, he continued, "As I look out today, I see this successful winery and this vast fortune I've managed to amass, yet look at my home. It's empty . . . and so quiet. How is it possible for one man to have so much, and also to have so little?"

It turns out that Hendricks burned a lot of bridges on his way up the ladder of material success. He alienated friends, neighbors, and even his own family. He poached workers from other local wine-makers and then didn't treat them well. He admitted that he had been arrogant and unattached to anything except his growing bank account.

His remorse was painful to hear. As I listened to him share his story and his regrets, I couldn't help but think about the giant house, the empty chairs, the white walls, and the tall ceilings. I wondered how long it had been since there was love, laughter, and joy in that home.

Hendricks acknowledged his material possessions were a facade, designed to make it look like his life was perfect. He craved fame and notoriety and wanted everyone to look up to him, but in the end, no one did. I was struck by his raw and honest way of sharing this revelation. "Maybe I was afraid . . . afraid of love, afraid of not being a success. I really don't know why I never put other people first, but I see now how selfish I was. I don't blame anyone but myself. I fucked up. I wasted so much time . . . time that I will never get back with my family or my friends . . . time I will never get back to travel, or take a long hike in the woods, or just to sit around a table and talk about the day."

He tried to reconnect with his family, but no one came. Hendricks died with a caregiver holding his hand.

Just a month after Hendricks died, I received a call from another client, named Steven. Although he didn't have a giant estate or a high-powered life, his experiences and emotions were very similar. Steven's wife and kids were in denial about his illness, and he was having a hard time pretending that he was going to live forever. We set up an appointment for later that week.

Steven worked in the wine business, too, often visiting restaurants and bars and attending events late into the nights and on weekends. Steven and his wife managed to save money each month, and when their third son was born, they moved out of an apartment and bought a small house in a cozy neighborhood where they still lived after thirty years.

On our very first phone call, Steven told me, "Back in the day, we were living the American Dream. It wasn't extravagant, but we had everything we needed, and we were happy. We had three sons and lots of friends. I had job security and a wife who loved me. But then life just got away from me." I always allow plenty of time for an initial client call because there's usually a lot of life that needs to be talked about, along with death and dying.

Within ten minutes of my meeting Steven in person, it became clear he was holding guilt and regret for how his work took over his life and for some of the choices he made. He said, "It's kind of crazy how fast the years went by. I kept getting promoted, and, every time I did, I ended up losing connection to my wife and kids. They were slowly slipping away. I didn't really pay attention, but when my oldest son killed himself, my world stopped."

He stared down at the worn carpet. This was hard for him to talk about, yet I could sense the tension releasing in his body. Sometimes people just need to tell their story to someone who won't judge them. It would've been easy for me to fill the gap with a question or a comment rather than sitting in the discomfort of silence, but I didn't. Quiet moments are fertile ground for truth and healing.

He took a deep breath and kept talking. "My wife is a saint. She is so strong. She took care of our other sons and me. She was devastated, but I was so focused on my own grief and guilt for not being home that I don't even remember hugging her or asking her how she was doing. What's worse is that I started working even more, burying my sadness, and doing everything I could to avoid the gaping hole in my heart. And I've never stopped . . . until now. If it wasn't for the Parkinson's disease, I'm certain I'd be there right now, working my ass off for a little overtime pay and the next promotion."

Steven, like many of us, didn't take the time to truly consider what would matter most in the end, until the end came calling. This is another thing that all of us humans share. We can't turn back the clock, and we can't replace time.

Unlike Hendricks, Steven had enough time to heal his hurting heart. He reconnected with his family and apologized for the years he spent prioritizing his work over everything else. There was forgiveness, and there was love and lightness in the home again.

His wife and the boys came to accept Steven's prognosis. They made memories and spent joyful hours with each other until Steven took his final breath, with his family by his side.

These stories echo the sentiment shared by many of my clients who feel they didn't make the best use of their precious time. Some chose work over family. Some chose money over memories. And then there was Lenny.

Lenny wanted to meet with me to make sure he "wasn't missing anything." He'd been living with multiple myeloma, a type of cancer in plasma cells, for six years. As his disease became more aggressive, so did Lenny's pain and suffering. His thinning bones led to a broken hip, and he suffered from anemia and ongoing kidney problems.

When we met in person, Lenny shared, "I'm no doctor and I'm no psychic, but this disease seems to be knocking me down faster than I can get back up. I've had a good life, and now I need to plan for a good death." He had recently enrolled with hospice and decided it was time to come to terms with the fact that the end was near. Right away, I admired his willingness to explore his life, uncover any potential unfinished business, and talk about any regrets.

Lenny was an insurance broker with a nationally known firm. He had a loving wife of forty-eight years, four children, nine grandchildren, and what seemed like an entire community of constant friends and visitors. I watched Lenny treat them all as if they were his best friend. It seemed that Lenny's mission in life was to make every person in his world feel special . . . especially his grandchildren.

Lenny took every Friday afternoon off from work. He worked late and on weekends to make up for it, but he never worked on Friday afternoons. That precious time was reserved for ice cream and grandkids. Instead of buying a second "flashy car," as Lenny called them, he bought a Ford twelve-passenger bus. Lenny, along with his wife and the weekly rotation of family chaperones, would take all nine grandkids for ice cream and an outing. Each grandchild had their own personal song, created by Lenny, that they all knew and sang along the way. It was Lenny's way of helping each one to feel special.

Relationships, family, community, and service mattered to Lenny, and he took time every day to foster those things that meant the most to him.

I met with Lenny once more, as he was nearing the end of his life. He knew what was most important to him. He didn't miss the moments. He didn't squander his time. Lenny was a rare client. He was one of the few who seemed to have figured out very early in his life what mattered most and then lived his life accordingly. Of course, he had regrets, but most were based on circumstances beyond his control, and he'd generally come to accept them as a result. Lenny had prioritized his relationships and had a clear understanding of his life's purpose and meaning.

Like my own Grandpa Charlie, Lenny died with a giant, gentle smile on his face. He made the most of his time on earth. He said everything he wanted to say, did everything he needed to do, and felt that pure love from his family, which helped him die in peace.

These stories are reminders to slow down, cherish your time, and be more thoughtful about the choices you make in life. They exemplify a truth, that relationships are more important than success or wealth, that joy comes from being present and living every moment to the fullest, and that how we choose to spend our time is one of the biggest choices we will ever make.

In truth, all of humanity is given a new opportunity each morning, a moment to hit the pause button, be still, and reflect on what matters. It takes time and thoughtful effort to cultivate and nurture a balanced, meaningful life. Take a moment when you first wake up to set an intention for your day, not based on success or productivity but based on who and what is most important to you and how you want to spend your precious time.

Lenny's story reminds me of the memorable words of another client named Ellen, a wise and wonderful forty-two-year-old woman who faced her death with such courage.

Right before Ellen died, she held my hand, looked me in the eye, and reminded me one final time, "You can replace anything in this world except for time and the people you love. Make the most of both of those, and you will live a wonderful life. Money comes and goes, but time only goes."

Those were her final words, a gift to all of us to remember that time is precious, so make the moments count. After all, the moments turn into hours, then the hours turn into days, which turn into weeks and then years, and soon they become a lifetime.

LESSON #15

Time only goes, so be sure to spend it wisely.

Show Up and Finish Well

A wise and observant client once said to me, "Some people are just assholes."

Being a doula is heartfelt work, but that doesn't mean that all our encounters are filled with love and peace. We always strive to be nonjudgmental, present, accepting, and calm. This means that when there is stress and chaos, we stay anchored in our peaceful presence. We don't get flustered. But just as in everyday life, sometimes there isn't anything we can do except bite our tongues and not react. Sometimes things are better left unsaid, even when you feel yourself exploding inside. No matter what, we always want to show up and finish well.

Our job starts with leaving our own problems behind and meeting our clients where they are. But what if "meeting them where they are" feels violating and wrong? What if it gets personal? Can we stay calm when the stress or anger turns toward us? We try to be compassionate and understanding, but, probably because we are human, we have a hard time holding it all in sometimes.

It happened to me with the Smith family, where I was challenged to the point that I wanted to give someone a giant piece of my mind, pack up my doula bag, and walk out the front door. I will never forget Dr. Smith and his family, whom I visited with my doula partner, Lori Goldwyn.

We always want to meet our medical aid in dying (MAID) clients in advance to get to know them, along with those who will be there on the day they ingest the medicine. We want to be sure the client is alert and aware, able to express the desire to end their life, and able to swallow two ounces of what we hear is the most bitter liquid you could ever drink within two minutes. We want to be sure everyone in attendance is supportive of our client's decision, and we want to answer any questions and concerns they may have.

Lori and I drove together to a lovely beachfront town to meet with Dr. Smith, a retired surgeon, and his family. We were greeted by three of his five children, Jane, Ellen, and Jonathon. Before we even got a chance to introduce ourselves, Jonathon began swearing and complaining. He complained about the medical field in general, our local hospital, the "assholes in charge" at hospice, and the "incompetent nurse" who had just left ten minutes before we arrived. He even complained about how we were dressed that day, apparently expecting us to be wearing nursing scrubs.

We were directed into the family room to meet Dr. Smith, who greeted us with a gentle nod. Before we could say hello, Jonathon told us where to sit and instructed us not to touch anything in the room. Even though it was freezing cold outside, he told us that it was rude of us to walk into a person's gathering space with our coats on, and to be sure not to do that when we returned. The conversation was unusually cold, and Lori and I left feeling unwelcome, rushed, and dismissed. I'd never felt this way as a doula. I was used to misdirected feelings and complicated ways of grieving, but usually people were still able to recognize that I was there to support them. Everyone had always been so grateful, but not this family.

As we walked to the door to let ourselves out, we overheard Jonathon say, "This whole thing is a total shit show!"

I thought silently to myself as I reached for the door, "Really, your sweet dad is so peaceful, people are gathered here to support you, and you think it's a shit show?" Lori and I closed the door quietly behind us and left.

We tried to encourage each other on the car ride home.

"This is a lot for the family."

"Maybe they're scared. This is such a strange and unusual thing to do."

"Jane seemed nice."

"He's losing his father. No wonder he's so upset."

Setting aside our frustration, we discussed plans for our return.

Two days later, Lori and I drove back to that same beachfront town and knocked on that same oversize carved wooden door. I thought I was feeling pretty good, until I looked down at the larger-than-life-size doormat that read, "Welcome!" I rolled my eyes at the irony and realized immediately that I was still feeling the effects of the rude encounter the other day. I quickly prayed for compassion.

Within seconds of stepping into the house, we could feel the tension. One of the children we hadn't yet met was having a heated phone conversation in the kitchen. Jonathon walked past us without a word. One of Dr. Smith's daughters greeted us and told us to wait by the door until she came back and took us to the kitchen so we could set down our supplies.

We went to check on our client, Dr. Smith. He was in bed and said he was glad to see us, but he didn't want any small talk or unnecessary conversation in the room . . . not with him . . . not with anyone. I appreciated and respected this clarity and intention. He wanted to be still and quiet, and we wanted that for him, too. These were going to be his final moments, and we would do our very best to honor his wishes.

Within minutes, Jonathon walked into the bedroom, followed by Jane, saying, "Jonathon, try to calm down!" Jonathon seemed used to being in charge and getting whatever he wanted. He looked over at me and said, "Why the hell is this taking so long? Get your shit together. That's what we're paying you for, damn it."

I wanted to remind him that his dad was listening and was about to die. I wanted to let him know that we had just arrived fifteen minutes before, and this was going to take a while. I wanted to tell him that it's not about the money and that we are happy to serve the dying whether we are being paid or not. I wanted to tell him that it wasn't appropriate for him to talk to me like that, but I looked straight at him for a moment. Total silence.

Lori and I were at the kitchen counter, preparing Dr. Smith's tray for ingestion, when Jonathon approached again. "So listen, I want to speed this up, do you understand me? Do your fucking job! If this doesn't happen soon, it will be your fault, and you won't be able to cash your fucking check! Just do it. Now!" He stormed off and clearly expected us to jump through hoops and endanger his dad so that Jonathon could make it to whatever he had to do that was so much more important.

I was having a hard time containing my words that day, but I stayed silent. My doula skills and the desire to focus on the well-being of his father kept me focused and calm.

I thought of the words of my wise client and reminded myself that some people are just assholes. I tried not to take it personally, but words are powerful things. Once you say them, you cannot put them back in your mouth. My clients teach me how to be a better person, even if their example is the opposite of how I want to show up in the world. Mental note to self: Don't be an asshole.

I was somewhat comforted when Dr. Smith apologized on behalf of the entire family: "Thank you for being here. And I'm sorry about the intensity. My family can be a bit much sometimes, so I hope you don't take it personally. It's not about you."

So true. It wasn't about me.

Dr. Smith took his medicine at 11:00 a.m. After about an hour of calm and slow breathing, he quietly took his final breath at 12:18 p.m. with Lori and me by his side. We wiped his face, combed his hair, and sat with him and waited for the hospice nurse to come and officially pronounce the death.

What happened next surprised me. While I was outside waiting for the mortuary to arrive, I had a moment to breathe, and I tried to relax. Instead, I got emotional, which I wasn't expecting. I've done a lot of my own work so that I can try to avoid any triggers that might affect my ability to show up fully for my clients. But standing outside in the cold, reflecting on the day, I found my heart racing and felt anger creeping in.

I remembered that a friend of mine used to tell her daughter, "Let it roll off your back, like a duck." It took me several deep breaths to figure out why I couldn't let this roll off my back.

It struck me that Jonathon reminded me of someone from an abusive relationship in my past. Only once in my entire adult life has anyone talked to me like Jonathon did, bringing up the feelings that come from being told you are worthless, stupid, unlovable, and useless. Lori came outside, too, so we talked about it. She was upset for different reasons, but all rooted in the same rude and insensitive commentary.

I told Lori how I was feeling, and she set us both straight with one short sentence. "Well, maybe, just maybe, it's not about you."

She and Dr. Smith were right. Jonathon was rude from the second he answered the door. This had nothing to do with me. It was one family's journey of love, grief, and loss, manifesting itself in reactions directed toward me because I was there at that time. I am not worthless, stupid, unlovable, and useless. None of those feelings are true, because what is really true is this: It's not about me!

Hearing it for the second time helped it sink in. I felt lighter and free. There was nothing for me to do except let it go. Life is hard enough without taking on other people's emotions, too.

I thought of Dr. Smith and the caring service we provided for him and his family that day. I remembered the reasons I went into this field and the many, many wonderful people and conversations I've had. I remembered that the most important thing I can do is to always show up and finish well, even if others are not doing the same.

Something that felt like peace mixed with relief settled inside me, and I let it go.

Soon the mortuary came, and we were able to leave. Jonathon had already left, just in time to make it to his staff meeting. He did not say thank you or goodbye to us.

Overall, it was an awful day. But the peace Dr. Smith felt at the end was worth showing up for.

LESSON #16

Show up and finish well. Do your best, even when others are not doing their best.

Holy Smokes!

Life and death are only one breath apart. I've been present for this transition countless times. We describe this part of our work as sitting vigil. It never feels like work, as these moments are truly sacred. In this transition, on the edge between life and what comes next, I've learned not to question the unexplainable visons and stories I've witnessed in those final moments . . . those otherworldly conversations and stories of recognition and sweet reunions.

In one case, emblematic of this phenomenon, my dear client opened her eyes wide and shouted twice, "Ancestors! Ancestors!" just before her final breath. She had been speaking about seeing her ancestors again with such enthusiasm, and when they appeared on her deathbed, she was overcome with emotion to see them. Of course, I couldn't see them, and her family couldn't see them, but my client saw them directly in front of her, sharing the room with us.

In our Western society, most people wish to be surrounded by loved ones at the end of life. But, of course, it doesn't always happen that way. People die suddenly, some die in their sleep, and others choose to die alone. However, based on the visions and dreams that the dying share with us, many of us who work with the dying have come to believe that actually, no one ever dies alone. As you transition from this world to the next, you can trust that you will be held and loved by those familiar faces who have died before you. This has brought immense comfort and reduced fear for many clients I've known.

Over the years, I've heard and witnessed many stories of dying people who are visited by deceased relatives, friends, acquaintances, coworkers, kind strangers, and beloved pets. While I've never seen these beings myself, I trust these visions to be real and undeniably powerful. I've seen the smiles and enthusiasm on the faces of the dying when they are reconnected with those who are there to welcome them into the realm of the unknown . . . the realm that exists in that liminal space between life and death. I've seen arms reaching out for hugs, and hands waving in recognition while calling the name of someone they see across the room. My greatest peace in doing this work comes from my belief that we are all carried over the threshold and into whatever we believe comes next by others who have gone before us. To me, it's the most poignant and beautiful part of dying.

Because of those who have reported back about these nearing-death visions, we know that relationships can be healed, and forgiveness can happen in those transitional moments. One of my clients found peace by reconnecting with his best friend, a fellow soldier, whom he had to leave dying on the battlefield. As he sat up with his arms outstretched, he cried, "I'm so sorry. I'm so, so sorry." The healing was immediate and pure. You could feel the energy release in the room, and love replaced the fear and agitation. The heavy weight of guilt and its pain had been forgiven and let go.

How comforting to know that healing is still possible after we leave this familiar life. Death gives life meaning. If we were to live forever, we might lose our motivation, as time would become irrelevant. What if death were something we welcomed and even embraced with curiosity?

When Scott's wife, Susan, called me, she said Scott was doing well, but knew that she would need some support in the future as his health declined. He was diagnosed with prostate cancer several years before, but it returned to his lymph nodes and bones, resulting in constant pain. Scott didn't want to burden his children, but he was beginning to need more care, and it was taking a toll on Susan. She was exhausted, her back was hurting from lifting him, and she hadn't slept through the night in weeks. It was clear to me that she needed a break.

In addition to some physical support, Susan also wanted someone for Scott to talk to about his fears. He didn't want to talk about dying, even though he had already been on hospice for four months and was having a hard time getting from the bed, to the bathroom, to the couch . . . the only places he went anymore. Scott seemed disconnected from his feelings. Susan knew him well, and she could feel the anxiety growing in them both.

At first I felt like I was imposing a bit, but Scott eventually warmed up to me. Their three children did, too, although initially they were a bit offended that I was invited into the home to care for their dad when they weren't. I understood why that hurt them, and thought that decision might bother me as well if I were in their position. When it's appropriate, I like to shine a light on what isn't being discussed.

When I mentioned it, the family was open to a conversation, so we all got together and talked about everyone's feelings. Within a couple of hours, we had a plan in place that would give everyone time with Scott and give Susan some much-needed respite. Even so, she almost never left the house, but just knowing she could put her head down and rest or take a shower made all the difference.

Twice a week they gathered for a family meal, even when Scott became bedridden and dinner took place surrounding his hospital bed. This became treasured time for the entire family. They shared stories from the days when Scott and Susan first met on a blind date. They reminisced about their childhood, going off to college, the weddings and partners, the dogs, the neighbors, holidays, favorite meals, and inside jokes.

But soon, Scott began to turn away from the physical world.

One day I came to visit, and Susan was waiting for me at the door. She seemed worried and said, "He's hallucinating and talking to the walls."

"How long has that been going on?" I asked her.

"It started last night. We were all sitting around the bed with Scott when suddenly he looked up toward the ceiling and said, 'Dad! Dad! Is it time to go fishing?' Scott was so clear and convincing that we all looked up at the ceiling, too, but obviously nobody was there."

Susan said Scott continued to reach out his arms with a smile on his face and talked to his dad about a fishing trip, then sat back and fell fast asleep.

I explained this is something very familiar to those of us who sit vigil with the dying and that Scott was likely having a nearing-death vision. His lack of agitation and the peaceful smile on his face were further confirmation.

"Has Scott's father died?" I asked.

"Yes, they were very close, almost like best friends, really. They were on a fishing trip about ten years ago when his dad had a sudden heart attack. They were in the middle of nowhere, staying in a cabin near the lake. When Scott woke up in the morning, he went to wake his dad up, but he was dead. It was really hard for Scott."

It sounded like he was seeing his father, who was coming to greet him, as many ancestors do. Scott was calm and comforted by these dreams, showing no signs of agitation or fear. It brought him peace. Once she understood, this brought Susan peace, too.

Later that week I came to visit Scott for a few hours so Susan could rest until the family arrived for dinner. Right away I could see that Scott had declined even more. Susan told me he had stopped eating and wasn't talking much, either, except for the "mumblings to strangers" and a few more conversations with his father.

I sat by Scott's bedside as he slept. Often this work is about simply being present with the stillness and the silence. Scott slept for almost two hours until he suddenly sat up, waved his right hand in the air, and then reached out his arms toward the end of the bed. He had a huge, excited smile of anticipation on his face, as if someone was running toward him. I didn't know who it was, but Scott sure did.

"Henry! Jacob! Holy smokes! Oh my God! Oh my God!"

I continued to sit quietly, not asking any questions, or doing anything to disturb his reunion with what seemed like familiar faces. I slowly picked up my journal and wrote the words "Henry and Jacob.

Holy smokes. Oh my God x 2." I always try to get the words written down exactly as soon as I hear them so I don't forget any details.

When Susan returned later that afternoon, I asked her, "Do you know two people named Henry and Jacob?"

Her jaw dropped. "Why do you ask?"

I told her what Scott said, word for word.

Then she told me the story behind it.

Scott was just a teenager when his life changed forever. He was driving with his two best friends, Henry and Jacob, while under the influence of both drugs and alcohol. They were on their way to meet some friends for a bonfire on a beach in Santa Cruz when Scott lost control of his car, swerving into another car at a very high speed, killing the other driver instantly. Somehow, Scott survived the crash with just a broken collarbone, but over the course of the next week, both of his friends died from their injuries.

It took Scott decades to forgive himself. He did everything right. He never drank or took drugs again. He joined AA and sponsored young people so they could get sober before anything tragic happened to them. He spent his life giving back, making amends to the families he hurt, and trying to find his way in life after everything he knew and dreamed about was shattered in a second on that warm summer night.

The kids showed up right as I was getting ready to leave, and Susan asked me to tell them the story, too. One of the kids shared, "That's wild. Whenever Dad sees the younger grandkids and they've grown a bit, he says, 'Holy smokes, you're getting so big,' and gives them a big hug."

I was grateful I wrote down the words exactly. "Holy smokes" turned out to be a meaningful part of the story, too.

Scott woke up in the middle of that night and told Susan that he loved her and that he was not afraid. She watched a single tear slip from his eye. Those were his final words. "I love you, my Susan." He died the next morning.

I'm grateful that we have stories of people who no longer fear death and instead have embraced the mystery. It gives me peace to hear so often that our ancestors show up to greet us with open arms to escort us on to whatever comes next. I hope it gives you peace as well.

LESSON #17

Death is a mystery, but you can find comfort believing that your loved ones will be there waiting for you at the threshold.

What Carries Us Through

Based on my interviews over the years, spirituality and faith are important pillars of a meaningful life. When we have a spiritual practice that sustains us, it brings us comfort and a sense of peace about yesterday, today, and tomorrow. It reduces our fears and gives us hope.

Some of my clients have a faith or belief system that has carried them through life, while others find themselves grappling with their thoughts and feelings about what they believe right up until their very last breath. In my experience, it is the most difficult, anxiety-producing issue that unprepared clients must face. It can bring either extreme emotional distress or a peace that surpasses all understanding. Your spiritual practice may be an essential and urgent component of your final journey at the end of life, but you may also discover that spirituality is a meaningful part of your daily life now. If there was one bit of advice I would give you about preparing your heart for your final days, I would say to find peace with whatever it is that you believe. And do it sooner rather than later.

There is no right answer here. Spirituality is deeply personal. It's also almost impossible to define in a way that will fit everyone. It's derived from spirit, something unseen. Spirituality informs how we look at the origin of humankind, how we define our purpose for being alive, and what we believe about what happens after we die. It's not about a specific religion, and it doesn't require a formal structure. Spirituality does not label me right, or you wrong. It's a way that we are each individually inspired to know God, a higher power, or a concept of the divine that is greater than ourselves. No matter what it is, defining what we believe can offer the inner peace that comes from a life well lived. It's a mindful, daily awareness of how you belong, how you interact with others, what makes you want to get up in the morning, and how you show up for life. A spiritual practice helps us to make sense of our existence and purpose and inspires us to live accordingly.

My clients have allowed me to understand the importance of contemplating what brings people the closest and most intimate connection to their higher power, or their definition of God. When you discover what makes you feel that way, do it. Whether it be a house of worship, a yoga class, tending the garden, taking a morning hike, playing the flute, or dancing, do it with all your heart and soul. Whatever you believe, make peace with it.

Many people think that discussions of spirituality and religion have to divide us. I find that at the end of life, when we are able to lean into these topics with curiosity and acceptance, they can actually bring us closer together. I've had clients who have spiritual beliefs and practices that I had never even heard of before. This never stopped us from developing a close and meaningful connection. There are many paths people choose toward the great unknown. Nobody was born with a guidebook to understand where we came from or where we're going.

When I ask my clients what brings spiritual peace in their lives, I see those many paths.

"Knowing that I'm part of a big, beautiful, and glorious universe that is so much bigger than me. This, to me, is God." *Jasmine, age 36*

"Religion was forced upon me as a child. It feels so good to have found my own way over the years." *Elliott, age 58*

"I am grateful to have so few regrets and to have been forgiven by anyone I may have hurt. Now I'm ready and curious to see what the next adventure will be." *Ezra, age 79*

"My spiritual belief tells me that I will be loved and guided into the afterlife by my ancestors. I will be safe, held, and welcomed with open arms into whatever awaits me on the other side. This brings me immeasurable peace and the strength to face each day." *Marilyn, age 96*

"I've spent the last decade working on my 'self' to be a vessel of compassion and love. Compassion is my spiritual practice. This is what I feel called to do in this lifetime, simply to be kind." *Jayden, age 48*

"I believe in the great reunion. I cannot wait to see my husband again. My faith gives me peace for today and hope for tomorrow." *Lee, age 96*

"Forgiveness, love, and my deep faith . . . that's what car-
ries me through."   *Behti, age 67*

One of my clients said, on her deathbed,

"This is so beautiful . . . and so warm. There is light, everywhere."   *Lomi, age 76*

One day our chaplain, Clarence, and I sat at the bedside of a
seventy-year-old woman named Ruth who was experiencing severe
distress and agitation. She was sitting up with her eyes open wide
and calling out, "Please forgive me! Please forgive me!" Then she
would lie back down and fall asleep, only to be woken just minutes
later with a look of terror on her face. After learning more about her
from her sister, Dorothy, we realized she was in spiritual distress,
feeling the fear of abandoning her religion years before.

Her sister shared that Ruth was raised in the Catholic Church.
Even as a young girl, she looked forward to Sunday Mass, Holy
Communion, and even to confession, a practice of privately confess-
ing your sins to a priest, something that Dorothy admittedly avoided.
Ruth was always willing to lead the family in prayer before meals
and sang in the church choir during high school; however, everything changed when she left for college and became "a wild hippie
child." She lost touch with her parents, her sister, and the church in
search of something new, something she never found.

Dorothy shared that Ruth had spent the past twenty years saying
she was "spiritually empty" and had wanted to return to her child-

hood faith again, but life got in the way. There was marriage, work, children, travel, weekend events, and housecleaning that kept her busy and kept her spiritual life on the back burner. As her health declined and she became housebound, she still longed to reconnect to the Catholic Church, but she never did. Ruth told Dorothy she was afraid she had waited too long. And then one day, Ruth slipped into a place where she could no longer speak in full sentences or express herself. All she could muster was "please forgive me."

After asking permission to touch her, Clarence and I each sat on one side of her bed. Clarence took her left hand, and I instinctively held her right hand and placed my other hand gently over her heart. I felt a huge sigh. We recited her familiar childhood prayers, and Clarence spoke to her with pure love. In the silence, I noticed that all three of us were breathing in unison. Ruth was calm, and I silently hoped she had found her way back to the spiritual foundation that brought her a sense of belonging in her younger years.

I felt the distress when we arrived, and I felt the peace when we left. It made me wonder how much different her life would have been if she had found that spiritual peace earlier and carried it with her throughout her life. We left the house that afternoon, and, before we got back to the office, we received a call that she had died.

This wasn't the first time I've witnessed someone make peace with their religion or their spiritual beliefs with only hours left to live. It's definitely possible to find healing and spiritual peace at the end of life, but why wait?

A dear and trusted colleague, Redwing Keyssar, has worked in end-of-life care for decades, as a registered nurse and a midwife to the dying. She has witnessed spiritual peace and spiritual agitation, and she will tell you that having a spiritual practice can be your compass, or your North Star, as life goes on.

One of Redwing's memorable clients, Frieda, had a Buddhist meditation practice her entire life. She was a master gardener who tended to her plants and flowers with a flow that matched the changing seasons and the passing of time. She had a spark for life and cultivated a circle of friends who she knew would be aligned with her intentions and wishes throughout her life, but especially at the time of her death. Redwing called her a "beautiful elder" with her flowing gray hair and wise, bright blue eyes. Frieda was deeply invested in the moment she was living in, and it showed.

Part of being present and spiritual for Frieda was to "practice dying" just as Plato taught his students to do in centuries past. She would pay close attention to each inhale and exhale, with particular attention to the exhale, knowing that one day she would exhale for the very last time.

At the age of eighty-seven, Frieda had a stroke that left her unable to live a full and vibrant life. She sensed her death was near, so she began to let go of the external world and turn inward, preparing herself for the great spiritual adventure of death. When it was her time to die, Frieda was surrounded with love, meditation, chanting, and music. She had planned her end-of-life moments as best she could, discussed it with her friends, and orchestrated it to be the death she imagined. Just as she was present for her living, she was present in her dying. Frieda lived and died with spiritual peace.

Spiritual peace lasts forever. During our lives we lose friends, jobs, our health, our youth, and our loved ones. It happens to us all.

This is inevitable. Someday we will let go of life itself. What remains in the end is our spiritual foundation.

What does spirituality mean to you? It's never too late to consider this question.

By beginning to pave the path of your spiritual foundation now, you empower yourself to walk through the rest of your life with a greater sense of peace. And like Frieda, every day we can all practice both living and dying, just by focusing on the miracle of our breath and the miracle of life itself. Make peace with your faith, whatever that means to you.

May we all find that right path, and that indescribable peace.

LESSON #18

Know what you believe. Spirituality is an important component of a meaningful life.

The Lasting Power
of Contentment

Candace has one goal. She doesn't want to die angry.

My work as a death doula has shown me that how people die is typically a reflection of how they lived. If they lived loud and opinionated, they will likely die loud and opinionated. If they were compassionate and graceful, they will likely die with compassion and grace. Generally, we find this to be true, but we cannot dismiss the possibility that a person can change up until the very last minute of their life. This is where hope lives for people like Candace, those who wish for a different ending to the story of their life.

Candace's concern about potentially dying angry was rooted in the inauthentic and disconnected way she had lived most of her life. She was taught early on that there was only one path to happiness, and looking back over the years, she was angry for living her entire life believing that to be true. Candace isn't alone in this belief. Many clients tell me they just want to be happy after years of living an unsatisfying life. That's a beautiful but lofty goal, as it is impossible to feel happy all the time. These statements make me wonder if contentment, the state of feeling satisfaction and peace with one's situation, might be a more realistic goal.

Contentment is still and calm. It is not seeking. It is accepting. It gets you through the moments when you can't access happiness, like during big life changes, such as a move or a divorce, or small ones, like discovering your favorite breakfast cereal has been discontinued. Maybe we don't feel in touch with our joy in those moments, or like there is even room for joy in our lives during unhappy times. But contentment can live alongside sadness, reminding us that there are still things that matter to us and give us meaning. It can carry us from one wave of happiness to the next, giving us strength and a sense of calm to cope with the lows that inevitably exist between the highs in our lives.

Contentment happens only when you are true to yourself instead of reacting to other people saying what you should do or telling you who you should be. To be true to yourself, you must go inward and listen to your own voice. It starts with an honest self-reflection. Trust that you know best. The next time you find yourself thinking, "I just want to be happy," ask yourself if you are living a life that is true to who you are, deep down in your core. It's so easy to lose our "true" selves in a world that calls us to seek external pleasures and fit into certain stereotypes, often at the expense of our internal peace. But we can reclaim our true selves when we pause, reflect, and accept who we are. You don't have to wait until you are dying to change your life and live authentically, with all the inner peace and contentment you deserve.

Candace was eager to find contentment. She needed to get back in touch with where she found her meaning, but first she had to look back and carefully examine who she was and who she wanted to be. She took the first step, which was to ask for support. She engaged the doula services of my friend and colleague Greg Brown, founder of Armonia Maxima, in Columbus, Ohio. Candace contacted Greg to talk about her life, which was her way of preparing for death. She needed someone to hear her painful story without trying to fix it or change it, but simply to listen and honor her end-of-life journey. Greg, who has a big heart and an easygoing presence, has supported many clients with his ability to listen and bear witness to their story. He is unwavering in his acceptance for all. He and Candace were a perfect fit.

Candace stated right up front that she had lived an unhappy life, and she wasn't looking for happiness anymore. Her life had shown her that happiness was temporary anyway, causing us to always look for the next extraordinary thing to make us happy again and again. Candace needed more than that. She needed to finally let go of the anger she was clinging to so she could heal from her past and finally experience true and lasting peace and contentment. She needed to finally be true to herself.

Greg helped Candace start her healing process by taking a deep dive into her past. She was raised by a self-absorbed mother and an abusive father. Her life was filled with emotional and physical pain, suffering, and unhealthy relationships. In her teenage years, she was admitted to a mental health hospital, where she stayed through most of high school.

She remembers those years as some of her better times, perhaps even with some fondness. It was the early 1970s, and times were different then. She found kindred spirits in the hospital, and even some caring adults. Candace helped many of the other young people, often those who were institutionalized only because they were gay or lesbian. Candace was the loving voice who assured those patients that they were lovable and good, and that there was nothing wrong with them except for the stigma that labeled them as defective.

In the hospital, Candace helped others get to know and love themselves, but she never took the time to do the same for herself, even after she was released. She hit the ground running, and life kept hitting her hard. One brother died by suicide, and another was diagnosed with a rare cancer at age twenty-four. Her mom developed dementia, and her father was long gone. Candace buried herself in work, saved money, met a man, got married, and had three kids. She bought a "normal" house in a friendly neighborhood, put up the white picket fence, and built a life that she hoped would sustain her and keep her safe.

There was just one problem. Candace was seriously unhappy and not living her truth in this fabricated, empty life. She was in a loveless marriage, and her now adult children were emotionally detached and not interested in acknowledging the sad truth that was lingering behind the facade of that white picket fence.

Candace had spent her life seeking what she had been taught to believe was the formula for happiness . . . the house, the husband, the kids, and the stereotypical signs of a "good life." But that didn't work. Yes, she found happiness in some moments, but they did not add up to a joyful or meaningful life for her. Candace had never given herself permission to explore what else a meaningful or contented life could look like, so it was hard to imagine any life that she could make for herself that could provide her with that. She spent decades not knowing who she truly was, going through the motions of living a life that was meant for someone else, someone Candace barely even recognized.

Many of us live life from the outside in, assessing ourselves and our behaviors through the judgment of others, then adjusting to align better with who we feel we are supposed to be. We think we will be happy when we fit in. But when we lose ourselves to be accepted by others, we also often lose our ability to connect with who we actually want to be. We must be able to turn inward to find the things that make us feel fulfilled and then continue to live our lives from the inside out. True contentment comes from within.

Decades passed before Candace finally paused long enough to reevaluate her life. By the time she met Greg, she was aging and frail. She was diagnosed with COPD and cancer, but it was the advancing dementia that was weighing heavily on her. It was time to get real. She finally allowed herself to become honest with the stories hidden inside her lonely heart, as well as the inauthentic life she was living on the outside. The stories didn't match. Candace's inner life was so much richer than her outer life . . . huge and vibrant and filled with dreams and adventures that never came to be.

Greg became that safe space for Candace to share her truth. She was finally able to say out loud that she was a lesbian and was married to a man who would never have the privilege, or care enough, to hear her inner story. In her numb and empty life, she had pushed away her children, didn't see her grandchildren, and avoided friends and social activities altogether. No one truly knew her, and she was very much alone. Candace wasn't seeking to blame others for the life she had created. At this point, the only acceptance she was seeking was from herself.

Greg asked her, "What are your goals for our time together?"

Candace replied, "I want to have a good death. I know I'm not going to be happy, but I want to be comfortable, and I want to be content. I want to be at peace with myself and my past."

Candace couldn't change the way she had lived her life, but she could let go of whom she'd been pretending to be in order to finally discover who she truly was.

Over several deep conversations it became clear that Candace had never been very kind to herself, which added yet one more difficult relationship in her life—the relationship she had with herself. She committed to changing this pattern, one of the few things she could control. She intended to find as much joy and contentment as possible for whatever time she had left.

Letting go of the past was about sharing her stories, sometimes over and over again. Candace found this to be a healing way of letting it out before letting it go. Story after story, Candace lightened her load and released a lifetime of shackles that tethered her to her tragic and inauthentic past.

Greg shared, "At that point in her life, Candace didn't have any unfinished business. She didn't need to ask for forgiveness from anyone. She'd never intentionally hurt people, and when she had, she's apologized. She felt comfortable that she'd done the best she could in her lifetime. There was nothing left unsaid. She's made her peace, and now she wants to live and die in a way that makes her most content, whether it be for one month or seven years."

According to Candace, she doesn't expect to experience many moments of happiness, and that's OK. She doesn't have the time, strength, or energy to change her story, to fall in love with the right person, or to foster relationships with those who have cast her aside. She lives alone, but she's content. She's honest and true to herself. She is no longer angry. It doesn't matter to Candace how much time she has left, because she is living every moment of it with all the contentment and joy that her hard-earned authenticity has gifted her. Contentment is the reward for authenticity.

And yes, Candace is dying, but today she's engrossed in her favorite books, with her cat on her lap, sipping a very fine and unforgettable cup of piping hot tea.

Try your best to always be true to yourself, starting today. Be sure that your passions, values, and intentions align with how you're living right now. When you are content with your life and yourself, you begin to notice when you have enough, and you find acceptance and satisfaction with the present moment. When you stop frantically searching for happiness, you can slow down and experience the beauty of the here and now. This is truly one of life's greatest gifts.

When we live with authenticity and contentment, it stays with us. It's longer lasting and much easier than working so hard to be happy all the time. It's that deep sense of goodness and peace that we carry in our hearts wherever we go. We don't have to seek it out, because it exists within us. Authenticity is restful, serene, uncomplicated, and grateful . . . just as your true self should be.

LESSON #19

*Be true to yourself. That is when you will
find contentment and inner peace.*

John, Paul, George, Ringo . . . and Ed

Our living spaces say a lot about us. When you look around, what makes you feel good? What brings back good memories? What brings you the most joy? These are your cherished possessions, and you will likely discover that it's not always the most expensive items that evoke the best feelings inside. You might be attached to a heart-shaped seashell or a rock you painted with your best friend. Maybe you have collected old keys, coins, or pieces of sea glass. The things that bring you joy are special, some of the first things you would grab if there were a fire or the last things you would give up if you were lightening your load.

Whatever you surround yourself with tells your personal story and shines a bright light on what you hold closest to your heart. Pay attention to what you are accumulating as the years go by, and make sure you are filling your life with items that are adding joy and meaning to your life.

One of my clients, an artist named Neha, drew pictures of the

San Francisco skyline with crayons, and included a color-coded graph of which crayons she used under each drawing. These huge pieces of art covered her tiny apartment like wallpaper. She always had crayons and paper available for anyone who stopped by and wanted to draw.

Another client, Keenan, told me his friends called him "bird man" because he had an entire wall filled with feathers he had collected over his lifetime, with colorful peacock feathers featured in the center. There is never a shortage of conversation topics if you simply ask to hear a story about a colorful piece of crayon art, a wall of mixed bird feathers, a collection of anything at all, or any framed photo.

While I love the stories about my clients' treasures, I personally don't tend to hold on to many things. I have seen so many clients at the end of their lives purging their homes of items they did not even know they had lying around, that I often find myself asking, "Will I really care about this when I'm ninety?" But when something does bring me joy, I remember a man named Ed, and I allow myself to be surrounded with the things that inspire me and make me feel good.

Ed was a fun-loving client and a die-hard Beatles fan. He collected life-size memorabilia, and Beatles art and photos covered his walls. He knew every word from every song, but not only that, he could tell you who wrote it and when, and the story behind all the lyrics. This was his passion, yet it also helped him to define so many other important aspects of his life, including who and what mattered most to him. I love the Beatles, too, so we had an immediate connection.

Usually, Ed told me how he was doing with just a short one-liner from a famous Beatles song, but sometimes he would reveal a lot more while belting out a few meaningful lines. It touched a soft spot in my heart one day when I heard Ed humming a familiar song as I approached his front door. I knocked, and he opened the door not with a greeting but with a song.

"Yesterday, all my troubles seemed so far away." He invited me in without missing a beat and I joined him in singing the rest of that verse. Whenever Ed sang, I paid special attention to what songs he chose and what their lyrics might have meant to him in that moment.

Even though I was a Beatles fan, I didn't know them as well as Ed, so I did some Beatles research on my own time to find some good comebacks. This would always make him smile because he knew we were both connected to George, Paul, John, and Ringo, and he felt safe. This connection would inevitably lead us to the best conversations.

My weekly visits with Ed lasted for eight months. Over time, as I learned to speak his music-infused language, I could respond with the best supportive advice I had. One day, in the middle of a conversation about the endless list of tasks he needed to finish around the house, I told him, "Don't carry the world upon your shoulders," and he looked at me with the biggest grin on his face. At that moment, I knew we had bonded.

During one visit, Ed said he'd been feeling lonely that week, so he made plans and went out for lunch and a game of mah-jongg with his old roommates. Though physically tired, he was feeling emotionally rejuvenated because he socialized with friends. He told a long story without any Beatles references, and I got a little concerned until he said, "Well, I learned a long time ago to ask for what I need, and that's how I get by with a little help from my friends."

Ed was a sixty-six-year-old widower who had been married three times. Ed's third wife, Tammy, shared his love of the Beatles and changed his opinion about relationships. He told me one day, "My first two wives taught me how to fight. My last wife taught me how to love. Tammy never held back her heart. She always wanted the best for me. When she was upset, we talked. We didn't yell. We didn't say hurtful things. We would always remember one of our favorite Beatles songs, look at each other with a grin, and say, 'We know how to work it out . . . ' and we always did. I miss her so much."

Tammy and Ed were diagnosed with cancer within two months of each other. She died a year before he did, and from the first moment I met Ed, it was clear that life had lost a lot of its glimmer and shine without Tammy.

Ed wiped a tear from his eyes and continued, "So many of my guy friends are afraid to fall in love, and when they do, they fight constantly. I don't get it. This is what life is all about, especially as we get older. Love is everything. Tammy showed me that all you really need to have a good life, or even a great life, is love."

The next time we spoke, Ed told me he had decided to give away most of his clothes and possessions. I was surprised, because I knew how much they all meant to him.

"It's time to say goodbye," Ed said with a tranquil yet sad tone in his voice.

"What do you mean?" I asked Ed, thinking he was saying goodbye to me.

"This won't be easy, but I feel like it's time to say goodbye to my treasures, including my Beatles collection. I feel good emotionally, and my body is going to do what it's going to do. So now it's time to lighten my physical load. It's not fair to leave all this for others to deal with. To me, it's been a lifelong passion, but to everyone else I know, it's just stuff. These treasures have added so much joy to my life, and it would feel so good to find someone else who would cherish them, too. Besides, I know what it all is worth, so I want to sell it . . . all of it."

Ed's mah-jongg friends came by one day with laptops and sticky notes to help him organize his memorabilia. They went through his boxes and shelves, figuring out the value of all the items. Ed invited me over, just to see all the treasures he had been talking about for months. I walked into the living room and saw a group of men gathered together in tears, sitting on the floor, surrounded by Beatles albums, T-shirts, and memorabilia. They made this experience a legacy project for Ed, asking how he acquired all these unique items. It turned into a day filled with sharing stories of Ed's journey through life.

Day after day, Ed let go of the photos, the statues, the albums, and the T-shirts. When all was said and done, Ed had enough money to buy new musical instruments for a local music program for at-risk youth.

Whenever I was about to leave, he would say, "You're doing good work, Diane. Keep it up. The world needs kindness, and it's never too late to imagine all the people, living life in peace." And then of course he couldn't help himself and had to sing the next line. That was the line that always hit my heart, maybe because he was dying, but also because he truly was a dreamer, and it touched my heart to think that he hoped that someday I would join him again. His voice was powerful and bold, but his gentle and calm body language and the look in his eyes told me that he really believed there was hope for a better world.

Ed gave me hope. He was dying, yet he was still planting seeds for the future. He wanted to leave the world better than he found it, for others to enjoy.

A couple of weeks before Ed died, he gathered the few albums and a pile of Beatles songbooks that he had saved and set them aside. This was the last of his collection, and eventually he wanted the teens in the music program to have them. But for the time being, he wanted to keep these remaining memories of his lifelong passion with him just a little bit longer.

Ed realized that he could still hold all his memories close to his heart with just a few of the pieces that really mattered to him. He found comfort and joy in having them in his final weeks. But even more than that, he took comfort in knowing his well-loved treasures were in good homes, belonging to true Beatles fans who would cherish them the way he had, and that the funds of those sales would go on to uplift other future Eds or even future Georges, Pauls, Johns, and Ringos. What truly mattered to him at the end were the passion and the joyful memories the Beatles had brought to his life. By sharing his collection, he found an opportunity to deepen that passion, and to imagine it living on in others.

In this final act of letting go, Ed took his love of music and passed it on to the younger generation. Perhaps a few of them may even be Beatles fans. This was Ed's legacy.

I wasn't there when Ed took his final breath, but I'm pretty sure I know what music was playing in the background.

LESSON #20

Surround yourself with things that bring you joy.

The Ordinary Is Everything

My clients often light up when talking about the good things in their lives. With genuine warmth and a smile, they tell me what they enjoy most and what they look forward to. When I first began this work, I had anticipated that families would focus their reminiscing on the "extraordinary" moments that we often work so hard to create, like weddings, promotions, and exotic vacations. I was surprised to find that, time and again, what people recount most with affection and gratitude are those simple pleasures of an ordinary day.

Here are some of the answers they have shared with me when asked what brings them everyday joy:

"When my two German shepherds jump on my bed."
Natalie, age 59

"My best friend, who I've known for fifty-eight years. She calls me every day at 10:00 a.m." *Jan, age 75*

"It's really no big deal, but when the tomatoes start popping up all over the vines, I feel like I created something beautiful."   *Anne, age 50*

"I love the view of the mountain, my favorite coffee mug, and sitting on the deck when the sun comes up."
Alan, age 42

"When the grandkids come to visit after school. I used to bake cookies with them, but now they bring them for me! Their smiles make my day."   *Elizabeth, age 85*

My clients' lives are generally not dictated by exhaustively busy schedules, and they're not waiting for just the right time to stop and smell the roses. The time is now, and they know that better than any of us.

The dying experience life differently, and you can, too. Start by paying attention to just one full day in your life. What are the things you do every single day that bring you joy and make you feel good?

One wealthy client, Bernice, who traveled the world and lived quite an extravagant life, shared what she was going to miss the most. "When I die, I'm going to miss . . . just this. Sitting here on my porch, savoring my morning bowl of steel-cut oatmeal, and listening to the birds. This is a beautiful moment. Aside from the time I spend with my kids, I don't need or want anything else."

Over the years, she came to understand that a truly joyful and meaningful life includes quiet time, a healthy lifestyle, plenty of sleep, a spiritual practice, everyday kindness, time shared with others, and fewer material possessions.

One day Bernice said to me, "Look at these walls. They are covered with all the biggest moments of my life." We had looked at these pictures before, but today Bernice seemed particularly deep in her thoughts. She pointed from one framed picture to the next. "Here's our wedding day. This was me on the New York Stock Exchange. These are my kids graduating from college. Isn't this nuts?"

I didn't quite understand. "It looks like you've had quite an amazing life."

"Yes, I have, but I wish I'd put different pictures on the wall. After all, I look at these several times . . . every single day."

She looked over at me and then back at the wall. "All these pictures are perfectly posed. Every one of them is an event. Look closely. We're all dressed up. We have makeup on, and our hair done so nicely. We're all smiling and staring ahead. This just isn't life. Life is so much deeper and richer than that!"

"What would you do differently?" I asked her, beginning to understand this was another client who was confronting the truth of how she portrayed her life for herself and others to see.

Bernice looked at me and replied, "If I could do it over again, I'd hang pictures of pajama parties with my friends, and with my family and our dog all cuddled on the couch for Sunday night movies. I'd hang photos with me in blue jeans and a tank top, with wild and messy hair after a motorcycle ride."

She slowly walked down the hallway, pointing to another family photo. "Look at this one. Matching outfits. Pressed clothes. I don't even own an iron! And look at Harley." She pointed to a black Labrador retriever, looking toward the camera along with the smiling group. "Even the dog is posing."

She continued, "Every Sunday, when the kids were young, we took Harley to a local lake and let him swim. He was always covered in mud, so we'd come home and hose him down. Sometimes the kids would use shampoo and it was such a mess, but it is such a fond memory. Those were the moments. That was my life. You know?"

"I get it. Sounds like it's the everyday parts of living you want to remember, like your morning bowl of oatmeal."

"Exactly!"

Before I left that day, I encouraged her to pull out some of those old, memorable photos from her everyday life and just enjoy looking at them.

The next time I visited, Bernice greeted me, took my arm, and walked me into her living room. "Look what I did!" she said joyfully.

Bernice had created a collage of small, worn photos, all tacked together on a spot on the wall where the sunlight shines the brightest, like a spotlight on her "real" life. It took two visits to hear all the stories those precious photos evoked. Turns out those ordinary days were her most priceless memories.

Another client, Jessica, was living with dementia for eight years. She sat quietly in her recliner, day after day, gazing out the window, pointing at cars driving by, and smiling when one of her cats ran across the yard. The doorbell startled Jessica, so my agreement with her husband and solo caregiver, Ben, was to tap gently on the window two times and then let myself in. One day I walked in to see Ben sitting closely beside her, holding her hand, and staring at it intently.

He looked up at me and said, "I used to always chase the big moments in life. I was never satisfied with what I had, always wanting more . . . more money, more possessions, more success. There was always something more important right around the corner. I never really stopped to enjoy my days. But now, this is my favorite pastime . . ."

After a pause, he stared back down at her hand cradled in his. He lovingly ran his thumb down her fingers, stopping over her wedding ring, and continued speaking very slowly. "I love to hold her hands. They are filled with a lifetime of our sweet memories. These hands have held our children, hugged strangers, cooked thousands of meals, played violin, built furniture, taught classes, and planted seeds that grew into beautiful flowers . . . and I'm sure if she could talk, she would remind me how many loads of laundry these hands have folded."

He chuckled a bit at his last comment and looked back up at me. I said, "It sounds like those hands have lived quite a full and beautiful life, Ben."

"They have . . . yes, these hands have lived. And not only that but now I have memorized every wrinkle and curve and the way her nails are so small and dainty, even though her hands are scarred and a little rough looking from a lifetime of caring for me and the kids. I realized that, even after sixty-two years together, I hadn't taken the time to really look at her beautiful hands."

It's the simple things that matter in life. The small things. The things we may not even notice when we are living life in the fast lane . . . like our hands and feet, or our unique fingerprints, or the infectious sound of our uncontrollable laughter.

Our simple, everyday conversations matter, too. It's easy to take an ordinary conversation for granted. I remember one client, Randall, who was frustrated with a growing problem. "Nearly everyone who comes into my bedroom to visit me is gloomy. They look sad, too, especially with their forced smiles. What happened to the ordinary greeting with a big hug, genuine smiles, and an exchange of upbeat and enthusiastic conversations about life? I miss that. Now everyone wants to know how I'm doing, if I'm sleeping, and what treatments I'm having. Don't they understand this is the last thing in the world I want to talk about? I want to talk about life, and love, and how everyone is doing. I want to reminisce and laugh, not sit here focused on the fact that I have cancer and I'm dying."

Randall and I spent the rest of that day reviewing what brings him the most joy . . . being together and sharing memories with friends and his family. He decided to be more selective about his visitors and limit his time with each person to twenty minutes to conserve his energy. We wrote this note and taped it to his door:

> *Yes, I have cancer.*
> *No, I am not dead.*
> *OK, now that we have had the*
> *"cancer conversation"*
> *please leave your sadness at the door*
> *and come on in!*
> *Please tell me about your life.*
> *Tell me a joke or a story.*
> *Share a memory of our lives together.*
> *I love you,*
> *Randall*

Randall's visits improved immediately. He laughed and cried listening to the long-forgotten stories his visitors shared. One friend reminded him of the handshake they made up in college, and they began doing it at each visit. A cousin shared the story about how Randall taught him a "very strange way" to tie his shoes when he was a little boy and Randall was thirteen. He showed Randall his tennis shoes and they both laughed, realizing they both still tie their shoes the exact same strange way, forty years later.

No one shared extravagant stories about accomplishments, success, material possessions, or money. Their stories were all about their time spent with Randall and how much fun they had just hanging out together in the comfortable moments of everyday life.

Randall got me thinking about my own ordinary days, the ones that pass both quickly and slowly, linking together to create a life. I remember being home day after day while recuperating from a mastectomy. I was tired, but somehow the ordinary moments were magnified and seared into my memory forever.

Every morning, my nine-year-old son, Jack, came into my bedroom at seven o'clock and gave me a hug before leaving for school. He would always ask me, "How was your day so far?" and I would always laugh because I hadn't even gotten out of bed yet. His optimism lifted my spirits. My eleven-year-old daughter, Carly, came home from school each day and shared details of every interaction she had with her friends, which always made me smile and gave me insight into her growing personality. That summer, my youngest daughter, Hannah, caught her first firefly, which she named Annabelle before letting her go. And every night, for the rest of that summer, she ran into my room with the jar clasped in her hands and excitedly claimed, "Look, Mom, Annabelle's back!" Even with the pain and suffering I was experiencing at the time, I couldn't help but feel the awesome gift of simplicity in the eyes of my children. If I'd been too busy with my normal, fast-paced life, I would've missed those sweet, ordinary moments.

Challenge yourself to slow down and pay attention to what you cherish about an ordinary day. Are you moving too fast, racing toward some goal, yet missing the beauty of your morning coffee or the nature you pass on your commute to work? Think about those things you do, every single day. What are your routines? What makes you feel good every time you do it? How do you find joy in an ordinary day?

LESSON #21

*It's the everyday moments that add together
to make a full and beautiful life.*

A Natural Painkiller

We often hear that laughter is the best medicine, so it should come as no surprise that as a death doula, I laugh often. We make space for any and all emotions to be present in the room as someone is dying, but people are often surprised when I tell them how much laughter I get to experience with my clients. Some people don't see a place for something as bright as laughter in what can feel like such a dark time and place, but humor is such a big part of who we are. Our everyday stories are often laced with gentle teasing, familiar jokes, pranks, and sarcasm. That's how many people like to live, so it makes sense that it is a part of how many people like to finish their lives as well.

Some of my favorite memories with clients are in the moments when they are surrounded by loved ones and tears suddenly turn to laughter. Almost every time we reach this moment, someone inevitably makes the same joke: "You're killing me," or "I'm dying of laughter over here." I often find myself wondering how it came to be that all of these different humans, from so many different walks of life, are all united through this one simple joke, and the resounding laughter of their loved ones around them. Why do we all do this?

Why do we as humans so love to invite joy and laughter to join us among our pain and tears? Maybe it is because laughter is a natural painkiller.

I remember one day I arrived at a client's house with a bit of a heavy heart. A young woman named Bella was dying, and her partner was having a hard time accepting that she was quickly slipping away. They asked me to come over to talk about their situation and how to make the most of the time they had left. These are always emotional and difficult conversations, but they are very important. I gathered my doula bag from my car and slowly made my way to the front door, preparing myself for a lot of tears and sadness. However, as I got closer to the house, I heard laughter . . . loud, uncontrollable laughter. Suddenly, I was laughing out loud as well, wondering what was waiting for me on the other side.

The laughter continued as I knocked on the door and entered Bella's house. It was quite a silly scene to step into. The family's golden retriever was sitting next to Bella on the bed with a stethoscope around his neck, howling and nipping at the oxygen pouring into Bella's nose. That medical equipment was critical for Bella's survival, but at that moment it belonged to "Dr. Biscuit" as he tended to Bella and her family in a completely different way.

It feels so good to laugh. Have you ever found yourself laughing so hard that you have forgotten what you were worried or angry about? Laughter leads to the release of endorphins in our brains. It can lighten the darkness and bring us all together, too. We all can benefit from laughing. For those who are suffering from physical pain, humor can help alleviate that as well.

I have no shortage of stories when it comes to the ways my clients have made me, themselves, and their family and friends laugh. One client asked every visitor to share a favorite joke when they entered his room. Another invited all her loved ones over for a "Linda Finally Tells the Truth Party," where she spent two solid hours admitting to "all the stupid things" she did over the course of her life, including never-before-seen photos and videos she'd been hiding for decades. My client Greg insisted on wearing a custom-made T-shirt with a note to the mortuary professionally printed on it that read "WAIT! I'm not dead yet!"

And then there are the lighthearted things that people might do, or ask a death doula to do for them, before they die. I've been asked to shred love letters and romantic photographs that a client had wrapped in plastic and hidden in the bottom of her cookie jar for decades. For a postmortem prank, one woman asked me to "short sheet" her husband's bed after she died, just like she used to do when they were newlyweds. She meticulously taught me how to fold the sheet back just so, so that when her husband got into bed that night, his legs would get stuck in the sheets, and she would be able to make him laugh one last time. I have personally thrown away all the underwear that belonged to one of my clients because she thought they were all old and ragged and she didn't want anyone to see them. This was, of course, after spending several minutes laughing hysterically as we tiptoed around the room debating the funniest possible places to hide them.

My clients and I laugh at things you might not normally think were funny when someone is dying, but they are. Humor is a big part of this work, and sometimes it's the glue that keeps everyone connected and aware that my client is still very much alive.

One of my most hilarious clients ever was Greg, only fifty-three and dying from ALS. His partner of many years, Priscilla, told me in no uncertain terms that they were looking for a doula who would be lighthearted and willing to laugh with them until the end. I was up for the job and looking forward to being in the presence of such a positive and joyful man.

When Greg first met my doula partner, Franck Battelli, and me, it was clear he wanted to be sure we were a good fit. He let us know in a very serious tone of voice that he had a few questions for us. Being used to my clients having lots of questions, I went right into business mode, inviting Greg to ask me anything at all.

"What's your favorite ice cream?" he asked firmly.

Franck answered instantly with something incredibly specific like honey lavender vanilla bean. He even had a favorite ice cream shop, and it was obvious that Greg was impressed. Then it was my turn. I couldn't think of anything exciting, so I chose maple cashew from Swensen's, the neighborhood ice cream parlor from my childhood. While my answer was clearly a little boring for Greg, I passed the test . . . barely.

"OK, next question. What's your favorite alcoholic beverage?"

"Scotch, specifically a peated single malt like Ardbeg or Laphroaig," Franck said without hesitation, and then proceeded to give Greg details that once again led to a vibrant and energetic conversation about their mutual love of fine whiskey.

Greg looked over at me and I just had to humbly confess that Chardonnay over ice was about as exciting as it gets for me. As he looked back at Franck, Greg laughed and joked that he wasn't sure he was on board with a doula who waters down her wine. Thankfully,

Franck immediately advocated for my sense of humor, told him I was a fantastic and qualified doula, and promised I would make up for these egregious shortcomings in other ways.

Our conversations started out funny and just got funnier.

I was in awe that someone could face death with such grace and hold the emotions of love, fear, anticipatory grief, peace, and more all simultaneously. As a matter of fact, he was so easygoing and relaxed that I asked him a couple of times if he was worried or holding anything inside that he wanted to talk about. He always said no, and I knew why. He had Priscilla. She was his rock and his safe space to work through whatever came up for him.

He loved her in a raw and pure way. And she loved him like that, too. They had a wonderful life together, filled with exciting careers, travel, and plenty of good friends. Greg enjoyed his life, from bike riding in the mornings to sipping some whiskey from his collection at night. They were living the good life, until it all fell apart with the ALS diagnosis that seemed to come from nowhere. Greg had to let go of many things he loved, one by one. But through it all, he never lost his sense of humor.

As time went on and Greg was no longer able to get out of bed, he knew that soon he would be letting go of the two things he loved the most, his beloved Priscilla and his precious and joyful life. They cherished their days and nights together, trying to have the "normal" experiences of home-cooked meals and a movie after dinner.

The day Greg died, Franck and I arrived at their beautiful loft in the heart of San Francisco. As I walked in, I noticed bright orange gift bags that read "Bon Voyage" on the table. I had no idea what was inside, and with Greg's lively personality, I knew better than to try to guess.

All of us who were there opened our bags to find a small bottle of tequila, some fancy chocolates "because well, life is just so much sweeter with chocolates," and a rainbow-colored, penis-shaped lollipop, because "sometimes life just sucks." There was also a hilarious letter from Greg, filled with raunchy poems, funny one-liners, and an expression of gratitude and appreciation for being there for him, in his life and in his death. It amazes me to this day that Greg spent several of his final hours on earth creating gift bags to give to all of us, but Priscilla told me they had so much fun putting them together, and that they of course laughed the entire time.

Greg reminded me that laughter truly is the best medicine. We shouldn't ever forget about that, even during hard times. He loved hard and he laughed hard. We can all benefit from doing that in our own lives. Humor connects us, helps us cope, alleviates tension, normalizes difficult situations, and keeps us in the present moment. So why wouldn't we laugh?

Greg's journey with ALS was not funny. It was long, sad, painful, scary, hard, unpredictable, and ruthless.

But Greg . . . now he was funny.

LESSON #22

*Laughter has the power to bring us connection
and healing, even in sad and difficult times.*

The Stories They Tell

Everyone leaves a legacy, even if they don't intend to. This is because more often than not your legacy is built by your character, the way you care for others, the values you live by, and the examples you set in your daily life. Regardless of your family, your achievements, or your outward successes, it's your words, actions, and choices that will affect your legacy, and you have the power to change your story as you change and grow throughout your life.

I first learned this lesson as a young adult through two family members. My Grandpa Charlie was my role model. More important than being a doctor who saved the lives of burn victims and those suffering from congenital disabilities, he was a gentle, humble, and kind man. When I met someone who knew my grandfather, there was never a hint of anything but pure goodness. His legacy was built on his work ethic, his compassionate heart, his generosity, his faith, and his commitment to make the world a better place for those whose lives he touched. I was so proud to be his granddaughter.

On the other hand, when my Aunt Marcella died in a skilled

nursing facility, the nurses described her as "a firecracker" and "cantankerous," and one nurse said she was "quite a unique and complex piece of work." What they really meant was that she was not a very nice person, and sadly, I agreed. My aunt spent most of her life angry and bitter at the world because she was in love with her sister's husband, my Grandpa Charlie, a man she could never have. She was known as someone who was difficult and saw flaws in every person and every aspect of her life. Her legacy was one of negativity.

It became clear to me early on that we build our legacy day by day, and sometimes even moment by moment and word by word. While my grandfather inspired me at a young age to be a person of character whose legacy was built upon a lifetime of healthy actions and positive choices, my Aunt Marcella left a legacy as someone who generally seemed miserable and dissatisfied with life. I remember the mental note I made to myself to never be like that.

Generations from now, what stories will they tell about you? What words will they use to describe you? How will they remember you? For my clients who have more time to explore their past, these questions evoke heartfelt feelings about how their memory will live on for future generations:

> "I want to leave this earth better than I found it. I think I did that in my own quiet way, even though the world doesn't know my name. At least I will leave a fingerprint, a reminder to those I love that I was here . . . and I cared."
>
> *Jack, age 94*

> "I hope people will remember me." *Joannie, age 73*

"I wonder how my grandkids will describe me and what they will say about me ten years from now."

Beatrice, age 80

"I hope to pass on the family traditions and recipes that my own grandmother passed down to me." *Inez, age 89*

"I need to make amends and heal my relationship with my two brothers. I don't think I can die in peace if I don't at least reach out and try. I'm terrified they will only remember the worst parts of me." *Bernie, age 81*

Your legacy is the imprint you leave on the world. While your legacy will live on in the future, it is based on how you live your life today. Very few people will fund hospital wings and donate millions for a cause they believe in, and that is not necessary for your legacy to be meaningful. It will depend on your everyday actions and the way you treated people. A wonderful legacy can be built with a loving heart, small acts of kindness, and a willingness to make a difference.

Maria was one of those clients who had a desire to leave a positive legacy of loving relationships, hard work, and dedication to the planet. She was beautiful, vibrant, and wildly in love with Dan. She was committed to protecting the environment and making a difference in the world. Maria worked tirelessly for twenty-five years with local government and nonprofit agencies to create environmentally sustainable, resilient, and healthy communities in the San Francisco Bay Area. She lived a full and meaningful life, and the contributions she made in her field were important to her.

The month before Maria and I spoke, her cancer was in remission. She felt strong and was enjoying her active life. Then, during one normal day, everything changed. She became lethargic and achy, and she just knew her cancer had returned. Within days she found herself once again in and out of the hospital for aggressive treatments. When she and her partner Dan called me, she felt she had plenty of time left but wanted to talk about her legacy.

On our first call, she shared that just three days before she had written a letter detailing her final wishes for Dan and a friend. She wanted me to read the document, too, so we could talk about the "emotional cracks" she might have avoided or neglected to think about. She was very intentional and wanted to finish her life as thoughtfully as she had lived it.

In the first paragraph of her letter, before discussing material possessions and practical matters, Maria expressed her most important wish and the reason she wanted to talk to me. She wrote to Dan and her best friend, "I'd like, first of all, for you not to forget me, and to keep my memory tucked away in a special place in your hearts."

This wish was made even more clear to me as we talked more about her handwritten "will" and she laughed about her misplaced and very personal journals. Once they were discovered, she wanted them given to her friend for safekeeping, even though she knew it was a "huge and cruel job to inflict on her." Maria's specific instructions were for her friend to keep the journals until she felt ready to "read through them all and extract the good and well-done parts from the embarrassing, stupid, and offensive parts." She was then instructed to keep the good parts and burn the bad parts. Maria also wanted certain cards and letters she saved from friends and loved ones over the years to be sent back to them as a reminder of their times spent together.

Maria and I met during COVID, and it had been almost a year since the pandemic began. She hadn't seen her friends and coworkers in a long time. She was unable to continue working because of the cancer and hadn't been social in many months. She missed everyone deeply. During one of our video calls, Maria wanted to talk about her memorial. She wanted me to remind Dan to ask the guests to share a meaningful memory or a personal story about their relationship with Maria at her funeral. I could feel her sadness as she said those words, and I asked her if she wanted to talk about what it feels like being isolated and unable to have visitors.

"I hadn't realized until I said it how much I miss everyone. It feels like I'm getting sicker by the day, and no one knows that, except a small handful of people. Everyone is going on with their lives, and they don't understand that I may be dying in a few months. And I'm realizing that, because of the pandemic, I may never see these people or even talk to them ever again." She was already wondering if others at work had moved on, or if her name was still spoken as part of the impressive and steady progress they were making on the projects that were near and dear to Maria's heart. I wanted to honor Maria's wishes, but didn't want to miss an opportunity, so I asked her, "Would it feel good for you to hear some of those stories now, rather than waiting for them to be spoken at your memorial?"

She was still for a moment, then looked at me and said, "I would love that so much." She gave me permission to work with Dan, and we immediately got started. I'll never forget the enthusiasm in Maria's voice and the trust she placed in me to make this living legacy project happen.

From that day on, emails filled her inbox and letters began arriving in the mail. And as the days passed, Maria became weaker and weaker. Soon she was no longer able to check her email or get out of bed. Her decline was rapid, but Dan knew how important Maria's legacy was to her, so he sat by her side and read the letters to her, night after night. He read stories to Maria about her work, about travel and good times, and about the impact Maria made on the environment, the community, and on the people whose lives she touched. Maria was well respected and loved, and now she was able to hear the words herself, all written with such heart and compassion.

Maria passed away a week later, only a couple of hours after we finally met in person. After she died, I spent a long and peaceful time sitting around the bed with Dan and Maria's friend as Dan shared stories about how they fell in love, trips they had taken, and the simple ways they loved living life together. As I waited for the mortuary to come and take Maria's body, I washed her face and closed her eyes. She was so, so beautiful.

Even though Maria died a lot sooner than anyone thought she would, I know her heart was filled to the brim with loving, sincere, profound, and meaningful memories. I believe Maria died knowing that her legacy was one of a powerful, intelligent, hardworking woman who loved fiercely, cared about our planet, and made a difference in the world. There was no doubt in my mind that she would never be forgotten.

While we are young and healthy, or even when we are middle-aged, we are mostly looking ahead at what's to come. We plan trips, talk about the future, and look forward to new things . . . maybe a new job, a new place to live, a new relationship, new silverware, or even new socks. When we get older and accept that we are closer to the end of life, something shifts, and we start looking back. We contemplate what was. The different jobs we've had, places we've lived, and relationships we've had become our life story. These are the moments that happened over our lives that brought us to today. Some we may want to forget, but many of our stories are meaningful, and, as death draws near, these legacy-building stories often rise to the top of the memory pile. Many of my clients simply want to be heard. They want me to listen carefully as they retell these stories. Other clients want to be sure their stories do not die with them, and for them, legacy work becomes urgent.

While many of my clients wait until close to the end of their lives to think about their legacy, remember that you can start to contemplate your own legacy now. Consider the fact that you are creating your legacy based on your daily actions, how you show up in the world, the words you speak, and how you choose to spend your time. You have a choice . . . you are building your legacy every day.

How will everyone remember you? What story do your footprints tell? Where have you left your fingerprints on the world? What legacy are you creating?

LESSON #23

*Take the time to consider how you want to be
remembered, and be that person now.*

Don't Waste Your Gratitude

Have you ever taken time to think about how you feel inside when someone thanks you? When someone says thank you to me, I feel it in my heart, and it makes me smile. A thank-you says so many things, like "I appreciate you," "I see your effort," "I value and respect you," and "you make a difference in my life." It is so simple to say and so uplifting to hear. Gratitude brightens everyone's day. It is a practice of appreciation, touching both the giver and the receiver.

Just like other forms of unfinished business, often the need to say "thank you" to those who have made a difference becomes even more important at the end of life. People who have lived with unspoken words, maybe even for decades, realize that time is running short to express themselves. There is often healing in these moments when we act on the realization.

One day I was sitting at the bedside of a client whom I had come to know very well. I was trying not to cry as I witnessed this beautiful young mom, surrounded by her family, about to take her final breath. Mari hadn't spoken for two days, and she was peaceful and still. Each person around the bed had their hands on Mari while sharing stories and memories. Sometimes they laughed, but mostly they cried.

Suddenly, Mari opened her eyes. She looked around the room, then paused and looked at her husband. "Thank you for being the love of my life," she said.

Then she went around the room, looking each person in the eye. "Thank you for being the sweetest daughter I could have ever imagined. You have added so much to my life.

"Thank you for being such a caring and kind son. I am so proud of you.

"Thank you for being my big sister and always making me feel special."

Then she looked over at me and said, "Thank you for being my friend."

And then I cried.

Mari never hesitated to share kind words of appreciation, but on her final day, these words deeply touched my heart. It wasn't just that she said thank you, but it was the way she completed each sentence with a specific offer of gratitude for each of us, including me. Mari inspired me to be more specific with my own words by clearly verbalizing what I am thankful for. So now I prefer to say "Thank you for holding the door for me" or "Thank you for helping me lift those boxes." It feels more meaningful when an act of kindness is named out loud.

Another client who embodied a heart of gratitude was a beloved piano teacher named Miss Sally, who devoted her life to bringing joy to children through music. She was also an avid kayaker and loved to hike in the mountains with her two German shepherds, Hartley and Bo. She was healthy in her mind, body, and spirit, yet she felt something was missing from her life.

"What inspired you to call a death doula?" I asked.

"My coworker Cedric did a life review with a death doula to talk about his past and make sure he was at peace with the choices he had made over the years. He said it added so much to his life and made him live differently, and I thought that sounded like exactly what I need right now. I'm thinking about retiring soon and taking an adventure, and I just wanted to talk it through."

We met on her back porch three days later. She set out two glasses, a pitcher of iced peppermint tea, and a bowl of grapes. She poured me a glass of the tea and immediately revealed what was on her mind. "I've put myself on the back burner of my own life . . . and now twenty years have gone by. I still have hobbies and interests, but everything feels so routine," she said.

Miss Sally had spent her adult life focusing on the desires and passions of others without paying much attention to her own personal needs. She supported her late husband's career and love for archery, following him to events around the country. She raised three children, all piano players, all involved in sports and musical theater, and now all living in faraway cities and building lives with families of their own.

"Now," said Miss Sally, "it's my turn. I've forgotten who I am and what I love to do. I've forgotten the dreams I used to have and what made me excited to get out of bed each morning. I'm a little nervous, but I'm hoping we can work together so maybe, just maybe, I could revive some of the dreams I let slip away many decades ago."

Her future looked bright. She planned to kick off her retirement with a six-month "break from life" to explore her own passions again. Her best friend would take care of her dogs and the details of life while she was away. Her trip would begin in a small town in the South of France, where she would live on a budget in a friend's apartment. While there, she would volunteer to teach piano lessons to local children and practice her French.

After that, she would see "where the wind blew" her. She was feeling free for the first time in years, yet there was a hesitation about leaving that she could not quite pinpoint. Our time together soon revealed that Sally had things left unsaid and a few things left undone. She wanted to work through some of these issues before she left town so she could have a clean slate and feel even more free to enjoy her time away, so that became the focus of her life review.

During each session, I noticed that Miss Sally was always brimming with gratitude. She felt gratitude for the life she was born into, the gift of music she had been blessed with, and the family she raised with ease, compared with many. She was grateful for her teachers, mentors, friends, and even for the man who broke her heart, or the one who fired her from a job back in the day for being "too assertive." She realized the hard times were stepping stones, just like the good times, all leading her to this moment in time where she was filled with a curiosity for what was left to come.

Sally then realized something profound. While she was always appreciative of the kindness she received from others, she hadn't often taken the time to express her gratitude. This was the missing piece in Sally's life. Looking back at all the goodness she had experienced helped her shine a light on what a wonderful life she had lived and how many people she loved.

Between our weekly meetings, she called or wrote letters to thank those who had a significant impact on her life. She was only sixty-two, so she was able to find some teachers from high school and college, a neighbor who taught her how to cook, some college friends she lost touch with, and even the guy who broke her heart. Some responded, some didn't, but that wasn't important. Miss Sally knew she was addressing some unfinished business in her life by sharing her unspoken gratitude, and that was what mattered most.

After eight sessions and lots of journaling, she completed her life review and felt a big burden was lifted. She needed to feel that her life was meaningful, and over these past months, that fact became crystal clear. She said, "When I put my head on my pillow at night, all is well with my soul, and I can say 'thank you' for yesterday, to-day, and tomorrow."

One Thursday afternoon, I pulled up and parked in front of Miss Sally's house for what I thought would be my last visit. We were meeting that final day to go over the work she did, how she forgave wholeheartedly, let go when she realized she was clinging, and rode the normal waves of ups and downs just like almost all of us do over the course of a lifetime. We were also going to talk about her plans for the upcoming vacation, and how she wanted to incorporate these new memories and realizations into her life.

When I arrived, Miss Sally was out front chatting with the mail-man. They seemed like old friends, laughing and relaxed. She waved goodbye as he walked away, and motioned to me to come on in.

As we sat in her backyard, I sensed this wild and unbounded joy mixed with something else, but I couldn't tell right away exactly what that something else was. After a quick update about her trip to the South of France, she told me she would probably be returning right after that first month away.

"Why?" I asked her, mildly stunned at how excited she seemed when I imagined this to be such a disappointment.

It turns out that her routine wellness appointment with her primary care physician and a mammogram unveiled that she had breast cancer. She had no symptoms, just a tiny pea-shaped nodule the doctor said had likely been there for quite some time. I know firsthand that a cancer diagnosis can bring up a lot of urgency and uncertainty, but Miss Sally seemed focused on gratitude for her big, beautiful life instead.

"I'll need surgery, but the doctor approved me to wait a month. So, I'm going to France! I'm going to keep living my dreams," she said again with pure joy.

When I had a similar cancer diagnosis many years ago, I remember feeling like all my plans and dreams came to a screeching halt, but Miss Sally was different. She only saw the blessing of the time she had been given. For Miss Sally, going to France with cancer was still getting to go to France.

As our conversation continued, I realized she had a long road ahead of her, and that the work we did was more important than I had realized for her right now. She thanked me repeatedly for patiently listening to all the stories of her life during the past two months. I was grateful, too. It's always such an inspiration to bear witness to a person who has the courage to dive into their past and take action to make their life better.

"It's been my pleasure, Miss Sally," I told her. And I meant it. I learn so much about myself just listening to people tell me their story.

"You know, this life review was the most meaningful thing I've done in years. It's prepared me to live, but it's also prepared me to die. I feel free, grateful, and ready for whatever life brings my way," Miss Sally said with such a sense of calm contentment. The timing was perfect. Life threw Miss Sally a curve ball, and she was ready for it.

We talked a bit more about her month in France, and I asked her what she was planning to do when she got home from her trip.

She smiled. "I thought I was done with my gratitude letters, but the other day I was chatting with the mailman, and when he walked away, I realized I'd never thanked him properly for delivering my mail to me for years and years, always cheery, always greeting me with a wave. I took him for granted and wanted him to know how much I appreciate him, so I told him today, right when you were pulling up.

"I also realized I've never properly and intentionally thanked the garbage man, the bank tellers, the grocery clerks, the veterinarians who care for my sweet dogs, my dental assistant, my neighbors, my hairdresser, and on and on.

"When I get home from France, I'm planning to write them all, or go visit them if I can. And for the rest of my life, I'm going to take the time to say 'thank you' for the big things and the little things. I can't wait to go to France, but I also can't wait to come home."

Miss Sally inspired me to begin a daily contemplation of the many things to be thankful for in my life. You might enjoy this simple exercise, too. Each night before bed, remember three things you are grateful for from the past, three things you are grateful for from today, and three things you are looking forward to in the future.

And every day, notice all the lovely, caring, generous people who make your life better, more comfortable, and easier. Take the time to say "thank you."

Hopefully, when you put your head on your pillow at night, all will be well with your soul, and you can say a heartfelt thank-you for yesterday, today, and tomorrow.

LESSON #24

Don't waste your gratitude by not expressing it.

The Importance of Letting Go

Why is it so hard to let go?" a client named Marilyn once asked me.

I explained with a favorite analogy about a deck of cards. "Most of us were born with a full deck of fifty-two cards. Each card is unique and adds meaning to life. We don't realize it at first, but they represent freedom, work, adventure, energy, love, and all the parts of life that we covet so much. We hold them close to our hearts, but over time, we begin to lose some cards. At first, we don't pay attention. Maybe we can't touch our toes anymore or stay up until midnight, but we are OK with that because it's subtle. But then we start feeling the bigger losses. We may lose our parents or people we love. We may have to let go of hopes and dreams that will never come to fruition. Our hips hurt and our backs hurt. There is no set order or timeline for the more obvious losses in life, but when they happen, we know we have just experienced the loss of one of our precious cards."

"I've lost a lot of cards, that's for sure," Marilyn said, nodding in agreement.

"I know you have, and you have let go with such grace and acceptance," I reminded her before continuing. "And then comes old age. At this time of life, most people are just like you. They have lost a lot of their cards, and the ones that remain are even more precious. They cling to their driver's license because, once they let it go, they know they will likely never get it back. Losing this card is a loss of freedom and independence, and it's huge. They cling to the ability to cook a meal, to walk with a friend, to digest food, and to live without a caregiver. Over time, they may be forced to let these cards go, too, and it hurts."

Letting go can be hard. One client told me she was holding on so tightly to the thought of being cured, and to each scan and test result, that she was anxious, tense, and afraid every day in between appointments. She felt the loss of many of her cards and was desperately searching for ways to hang on to the few that remained. After a scan revealed there were no more treatment options available, my client was referred to palliative care, a growing field of specialized medical care for people living with a serious illness.

Palliative care teams focus on providing relief from the symptoms and stress of illness based on the needs of the patient, not solely on the patient's prognosis. What this means is that, while pain and symptom management is a critical piece, palliative care is really all about optimizing quality of life for both the patient and the family, based on the cards that remain.

When I work with our local palliative care doctor, Joshua Biddle, his patients often tell me they dearly love him, and I think it's mostly because he truly listens. He knows he cannot "fix" a person who is dying, but he shows up wholeheartedly to bear witness to a patient by offering kind and genuine support after fully understanding his patient's goals and needs. His job is to treat the whole person, perhaps beginning with addressing physical pain and suffering, but also expanding to address his patient's emotional, spiritual, and existential well-being. He wants to know what cards his patients are still holding and how they can make the most of the time they have left.

One way Dr. Biddle begins to understand his patients is by asking a few good questions about their lives and how they are navigating all the changes that came along with their diagnosis. The answers to these questions guide him, and they can guide us, too.

"What are some things that matter most to you right now?"

"What are your biggest worries or concerns?"

"Where do you turn when you are navigating hard things?"

"What would make you more comfortable?"

"What are your sources of strength or hope?"

These are reflective questions that you can ask yourself today, too. Most often quality of life is determined by the ability to accept the cards someone has lost while also living as fully as possible with the cards they have left.

Think about your own life. Are you holding precious cards that you cherish, or are you holding on to habits, outcomes, or expectations that are no longer serving you? Is there something you are clinging to with such brute strength that you cannot imagine opening your hands and releasing it? What if you could soften your grip just a little, just enough to relax a bit? If you have the courage to open your hand, you might feel a giant release and open yourself to a world of new possibilities.

Learning to let go of small things gets us ready for when the time comes to let go of the bigger things. Many of my clients work on letting go of some of those bigger things up until their final weeks or days of life. Usually, it's something emotional, and often something they've been holding for a long time, such as anger, fear, power, control, resentment, unforgiveness, jealousy, betrayal, or words left unsaid. These emotions usually trace back to incomplete stories, often about unfulfilled dreams or relationships that are still left unhealed.

Marilyn was ninety-six years old when she asked me to be her death doula. She wanted to die well, and she was willing and even excited to do the work to make that happen. She was a curious person, learning and studying up until days before her death. At first, she wondered why she was still alive, but soon she realized there was a reason. When I look back, my journey with Marilyn was a master class in letting go.

Over the years, Marilyn paid attention to her losses. One such loss was her youthful beauty. Her hair had thinned, and her once radiant skin had lost its glow. While it wasn't easy, Marilyn finally accepted the inevitable and even embraced it. She learned she could still feel beautiful with a bright scarf and a colorful, matching hat. This became her signature look. I thought she was stunningly beautiful, and I wasn't the only one. The ninety-year-old man who lived across the hall from Marilyn had a huge crush on her. He constantly brought her articles from the newspaper and small treats, just to get a chance to see her.

Marilyn's quick wit and eager spirit made her even more beautiful. Through the process of a life review, she began letting go of the burdens from her past, one by one. By opening her fists and trusting the process of letting go, she replaced her negative emotions with acceptance. When I looked into Marilyn's eyes, I saw her peaceful spirit.

After months of working together, Marilyn said, "This is cathartic. Looking back, it's clear I've been letting go quite a lot these past few years. I've let go of my driver's license and most of my independence, and now I only have a few cards. My cards are precious, but that's made it more clear that other things are not worth holding any longer." She was so determined that she actively kept a list of all she was clinging to and everything she wanted to let go of before her death. She narrowed the list down to just a couple of items that still tugged at her heart. We were making progress, but we weren't quite done.

One day I visited Marilyn, and she was even more upbeat than usual and had a renewed energy about her. Her large pile of papers had dwindled to a few key documents, and I noticed some boxes scattered around her apartment.

"You look perky today! And it looks like you've been productive, too," I commented.

She told me that her daughter, Jan, had spent the past few weeks with her, going through boxes and paperwork that she collected over the years. This was more letting go. Marilyn was lightening her emotional load, and her physical load, too.

"I just realized I only have a couple of things left that I want to let go of. I don't think this is going to be easy, but I'm ready!" said Marilyn, with her infectious enthusiasm and curiosity. Marilyn explained that she was holding on to the possibility of healing some relationships that had ended many years before. She had hoped to find healing in person, but realized this was not going to be the case. She needed to let go and heal by herself.

That day, Marilyn and I did a visualization exercise, which is like a personalized guided meditation. She first imagined herself as a little girl and smiled at the vision. She gave herself a big hug for being brave and kind, and for living with such integrity throughout her life. At one point, I asked her to imagine herself sleeping, and I saw a sweet, gentle smile come over her face.

As we continued, other stories from Marilyn's past rose to the surface, and she slowly let go of what was burdening her. She was able to find some healing by realizing that we are all wounded and imperfect, and sometimes people who are hurting can hurt other people, including those they love the most. Where there was anger, Marilyn imagined that person sleeping, just like her, which brought her an understanding of our shared humanity. Where there was hurt, she imagined them suffering, which brought her compassion.

"I feel so much better, Diane. We all have broken pieces and invisible scars, don't we?"

"Yes, we do."

"It sure is hard to stay angry at someone when you imagine them sleeping," Marilyn commented.

After spending a year and a half as her death doula, Marilyn became my friend and my teacher, too. She taught me a lot about letting go. I witnessed her unclench her fists and settle into a place of pure and wholesome acceptance. When she died, she was holding her two most precious cards, her enduring Jewish faith and the hands of her sweet family.

When your fist is clenched, you are holding something tightly. It might be an outcome, an emotion, an idea, a relationship, a possession, or a judgment you just can't let go of. Whatever is festering inside those clenched fists is likely not serving you well. It may be weighing you down, or even worse, making you emotionally or physically sick.

With clenched fists, we cling on. With open palms, we let go. Life is full of peaks and valleys, and throughout our lives, we are constantly holding on and letting go. This is the nature of life.

LESSON #25

Hold on to what matters. Let go of
what is no longer serving you.

Don't Wait. Say the Words.

Our busy lives can be detrimental to our human connections. Just as we rush through our days, we often rush through conversations with those we love most. Multitasking means that we are never 100 percent present with just one thing. We get distracted easily and don't focus on what is most essential and meaningful to say.

What if we all spoke to each other as if it were the last chance to tell someone about the difference they made in our lives? If we did speak those words rather than keeping them buried inside, people would know how we feel about them, and our connections could be much stronger.

Words matter. They are powerful expressions of our hearts, our minds, and our souls. So many of my clients tell me profound, beautiful things about their loved ones, and when I ask whether they have shared those thoughts or would like to write them down for me to share after they are gone, they often reply, "I'm sure they already know," or "It goes without saying." You would be surprised how often these assumptions turn out to be wrong. If you don't speak the words in your heart now, you may find they're still there years later, still waiting to be said. And sometimes, it's too late.

Take, for example, Evelyn. Evelyn was a caring woman, but her family would say that she had always been stubborn and was known for speaking her mind when she was upset. They knew and accepted her as she was, but over the past few visits, she and her young adult grandchildren had begun to argue because of Evelyn's strong opinions.

My daughter Hannah and I were her doulas. Hannah is a mental health professional and was there to offer emotional support to the grandchildren, who had returned to say their final goodbyes. They let us know where they would be waiting, hugged each other, and left us to sit with their grandmother. None of them could bear to stay in the room as she was dying.

With Hannah and I holding her hand, she told us about each of her grandchildren. The last person she mentioned was her grandson Todd, who was out taking a walk. "Todd is special," Evelyn began. "He is strong, smart, kind, and he has always been so thoughtful. He visits and calls me regularly, even though he has been busy with college and now his new job as a software engineer." She pointed at a picture on the wall and said, "That's him right there, the handsome one with the big smile. I'm going to miss him. I sure wish I could live to see all the amazing things he will accomplish in his life."

Evelyn died later that morning. Hannah went outside to check on the grandkids and tell them that their grandmother had passed. She found Todd sitting on the curb outside and sat down next to him.

Hannah shared, "Your grandmother sure was proud of you, Todd, and so grateful for all the phone calls and visits from you over the years. Her last words were about how much she loves you, how much you've accomplished, how kind you are, and how much she is going to miss seeing everything you are going to achieve in your lifetime."

Todd looked perplexed. "Really, she said that? She never said anything like that to me." Todd seemed somewhat hurt but was also smiling and told Hannah that it was nice to know that she felt that way.

Hannah and Todd sat silently, both understanding the weight of the fact that Hannah was the messenger of those final unspoken words.

It's always so touching to bear witness to those intimate bedside conversations where precious words that have been unspoken for decades, and sometimes even for generations are shared. Healing can take place in the final days or moments of life, but I can't help but think about all the time that was lost and all the opportunities that were missed along the way to say the words, to grow, and to share life. There is a better path. Whenever you have an opportunity to tell someone how you feel about them, do it. It will feel good for the person you tell, and it will feel good for you, too.

On rare occasions, I meet someone who has lived their life speaking their heart and sharing their words. They often have an easier time at the end. George Lee was one of those intentional people who did not leave the important words left unsaid.

George had a strong faith-based life since his early twenties. He was a veteran of World War II and later became an Episcopal priest, but in his heart, he was a community organizer, always being an outspoken voice for the underdog. His priority was improving the lives of underserved and marginalized people. And he did.

Even at the age of ninety-four, George attended a meeting with two hundred neighbors to oppose a proposed dam project. When the time was right, George went to the microphone and said, "My name is George Lee. I am ninety-four years old, and I should be in bed." The crowd cheered, and then George made the case against the proposed project. As long as George could speak out, he did.

George also made sure to speak out within his own family, too. He was married to Grace, the love of his life, for forty-two years. They had five children and five grandchildren. They thoughtfully created a multigenerational home and enjoyed having family nearby. I admired their deep family ties and the quality time they spent together. He never missed an opportunity to tell his family all the things he cherished about them. Healthy communication was important to George, and all of his family members knew how much they meant to him.

The last time I saw George Lee was on a rainy day at his home in Palolo Valley on Oahu. His hospital bed looked out to the moss-covered trees, and the slatted windows welcomed a fresh breeze and the sound of water rippling from the creek below. My husband, Mark, and I walked in and saw George's son Jeff, sitting at the end of his father's bed, strumming his guitar and singing George's favorite song, "Hawaiian Lullaby." It's my favorite Hawaiian song, too, and it took all the strength I had not to burst out in tears feeling the loving energy in the room while listening to Jeff's sweet song.

We didn't stay long. Family was a priority, and we didn't want to take too much of his precious time. George was calm and filled with gratitude. He seemed fearless.

The day before he died, George told Grace, "I think I'm going to die tomorrow. Is that OK?" Grace was taken aback, but said, "OK," with a bit of hesitation in her voice, not exactly knowing how to respond to a comment like that.

That night George's daughter Carol was wiping his face and getting him ready for bed when George said, "I just want you to know, I'll be leaving you tomorrow." Carol was surprised but George was sleepy, so she gently hugged him and whispered, "I love you."

The next morning, George told his son-in-law, Pete, in a matter-of-fact voice, "I'm going to die today."

George was ready. Everyone was ready. Carol shared, "When he passed that night, it was so incredibly sad, but it was also so joyful. There was so much love and so many sweet words."

George died the way that he lived, with nothing left unsaid.

Don't let the words in your heart die unspoken. We must take the time to speak our words into existence in order to give them meaning. Tell people they have made your life beautiful. And always say goodbye as if it's for the last time.

If you share your heart as you go through your life, you're likely to avoid a lot of urgency at the end. Don't hold back. Don't wait. Say the words.

LESSON #26

*Make sure those who matter most to you
know how you feel about them.*

The Final Checklist

This past New Year's Eve, our family gathered at home to play games and talk about the year ahead. Our oldest daughter, Carly, is getting her doctorate in counseling psychology and is a fan of stoicism and existential psychology. Her passion inevitably leads us to deep conversations about the meaning and purpose of life, and an exploration of the age-old question, "Why are we here?" If you are looking for lighthearted conversations, don't come to my house on New Year's Eve.

An hour before midnight, Carly invited us to complete an exercise to contemplate our priorities and hopes for the next year.

We all looked at each other, knowing we were in for a deep personal dive, while Carly went to the kitchen and gathered some small, matching bowls. She set them on the table and handed us each a piece of stationery and a pen while explaining the exercise.

She said, "I always ask myself if my cups are full. There is my health and fitness cup, my spiritual cup, and my relationships cup. Then there's my emotional wellness cup, my social cup, my career cup, and my financial security cup. They are all so important. I've recently added a new one, my peace and calm cup.

"Imagine these cups hold all your emotions and are guides to understanding your overall well-being. Which of your cups are empty . . . or low? Which cups are overflowing or may be getting too much of your precious time and energy? Which cups have you not paid attention to for a long time, and which ones are full and right where they need to be?"

Carly played some peaceful music, giving us half an hour to write our responses to her questions on the stationery. One by one, we shared our thoughts and self-discoveries, pausing to dig into the areas that needed some special tending this coming year. In this simple exercise, I explored my priorities, noticing that with time, my cups had shifted. I considered the cups that mattered most and what I might want to change to create more balance in my life.

I smiled the next morning while pouring my coffee. "Thank God this cup is full," I thought to myself. I began to reflect on my answers to the "cups exercise" and how the fullness of each cup changed over time.

As I read my notes on a client I was seeing the next day, I wondered about her cups. I thought about those who are dying and the way our cups may change when death looms near. The health and fitness cup might be slowly emptying. The spiritual cup may be filling, along with the relationship cup. Yet the social cup is often quite low. Career and maybe even financial cups become less relevant. Emotional wellness becomes critical, and, in those final days, the hope is that the peace and calm cup is overflowing and abundant.

My doula colleague Dr. Virginia Chang had a client named Nathan who was desperately trying to fill some of his cups before time ran out. In his case, this nearly impossible task was heartbreaking.

At the age of fifty-two, Nathan was living a "full and normal" life until he noticed a slight shake in his left hand. He was stunned when his doctor told him he had ALS. By the time he met Virginia, four years later, he had already lost his ability to speak and needed to use a wheelchair, and his hands were locked like claws. He couldn't take care of himself in any way. He was living in a studio apartment with his mom and a full-time caregiver always nearby.

The only way Nathan could communicate was by supporting one hand on top of the other, and slowly tapping out words on a tiny phone, using only one knuckle. This one-knuckle method was an exceedingly slow and painstaking process. It took so much time to communicate just one single thought. This problem was magnified because Nathan had a lot left to say.

The work of settling and making peace with unfinished business is already hard, but clients like Nathan who wait too long to do it often find it even more challenging and frustrating. It can be very hard to find meaning, peace, and acceptance when there is still so much work left undone and time is running short. People often wait too long to call hospice or a death doula, perhaps because they just don't want to think about it or accept that it's happening. In truth, involving end-of-life care can add to the quality of their time remaining and often even extend it.

Through this typing method, Virginia patiently learned to communicate with Nathan, helping him to express what he needed to say with the time he had left. Nathan had a lot of unfinished business and regrets about past relationships. Trapped in his body and alone with his thoughts, he often wrote to Virginia in the middle of the night. One night, he wrote her a four-page, single-spaced letter, typed with that one left knuckle. The beginning said it all, and Virginia knew that healing these past relationships was becoming urgent for him.

Dear Virginia,

I feel like I'm dying too young. The fact that there is no explanation and no cure, even in this day and age, makes me feel powerless and angry. I am afraid to die, but if I keep reminding myself about my connection to nature and the interconnectedness of all things . . . well, then I think I can face it. I have no choice.

I always thought I would have more time. I never had a great love in my life. In many ways, interpersonally, I've always felt like a late bloomer. And having been physically healthy all my adult life, I presumed I would live easily into my seventies or eighties. And I took great comfort in that, especially since I hadn't yet found a lifelong partner. So, to have all those hopes and dreams ripped out from under me has been hard.

Although the vast majority of my friends have risen to the challenge created by my illness, a number have drifted away, which makes me sad. I am seeking a sense of acceptance. Knowing that my time is short has helped me appreciate how beautiful the world is, in spite of the pain and frustration that follows me each day.

> *To the extent possible, I have also been wanting to*
> *create some sense of closure for my life. Since not long*
> *after my diagnosis, I have spoken to my current friends*
> *about the hope I have to reconnect to old friends who*
> *I have long ago lost touch with. The goal would be*
> *simply to say, "Thank you for being part of my life."*

With a cup of hot tea, Virginia sat at her desk and read Nathan's letter the next morning. She knew this must have taken Nathan all night to write, choosing every letter and every word very carefully. She tried to imagine herself in his situation and wondered, "If I were alone, even for just one day, without being able to speak or move, what would I be feeling? What would I be thinking about? If I were trapped in my body, with a heart that is feeling and a brain that is fully functioning, what would I write with my one left knuckle at four o'clock in the morning?"

It's a lot to imagine.

My guess is that whatever you would type in the middle of the night would help you identify or answer one of the six questions from an exercise I created to help my clients in their end-of-life work, called the Final Checklist. These questions have all been addressed within the pages of this book. As you review these questions, ask yourself how you would answer them. You don't need to be dying or to have a terminal illness to contemplate them. These are questions for you to answer starting today, and on a regular basis throughout your life. You might even urgently need to consider one of them now.

1. Who matters most?

2. What matters most?

3. What worries you when lying awake in bed at night?

4. What brings you joy when you are awake in the daytime?

5. What is left unsaid?

6. What is left undone?

While these questions may be simple, they are prompts to help us dig deeper into the core of how to live our lives. When working with end-of-life clients, doulas use these questions to help us discover any worries, regrets, fears, or unfinished business our clients may be carrying. They will highlight past experiences where forgiveness might still be an issue. Their answers tell me if they are at peace and if they have come to terms with their own definition of spirituality. They reveal what my clients still want and need to do with the precious time they have left. They tell me what is meaningful to them, and they tell me whom they love.

Nathan's story motivated Virginia to pause and contemplate these questions herself, reflecting on how prepared she is in her own life. Perhaps these questions will guide you, too.

Virginia and Nathan sent letters and reached out to his friends, but he simply had too much work to do. He did not hear back from everyone and was especially disheartened about one relationship that ended badly. He wrote Virginia one day, "I guess I will never have closure with this . . . and it's my most important relationship . . . my deepest regret."

Virginia guided Nathan toward acceptance. She explained, "The purpose of closure is to say what you need to say, not necessarily to get to hear what you want to hear. Writing this out is about offering you an opportunity to feel a sense of release for having said what you need to say, knowing you've been burdened with this for years."

Sadly, time ran out for Nathan. His typed-out words couldn't keep up with the work he still wanted to get done. He just didn't have the time and ability to communicate all that he wanted to say.

Nathan's story is a testament to all of us and a call to action. It's not an uncommon story. I've witnessed this many times in different circumstances. It's the reason I use the Final Checklist with so many clients, and regularly with myself. You can start asking yourself these questions today. Make them the heart of your journal entries, or use them every month to keep a clean slate in your life and avoid the distress that can come from years of accumulating unresolved issues.

Ask yourself who matters most, what matters most, what brings you joy, what causes you to worry, what is left unsaid, and what is left undone. And to help you heal through any hard times, ask yourself what brings you comfort and what brings you peace.

Some of my clients have said, "I wish I knew about the Final Checklist years ago. I would've lived differently, and I might have loved differently, too." Sadly, they cannot go back and change their lives. However, their stories have the power to change yours.

LESSON #27

*Contemplate life's important questions now so
there is little unfinished business at the end.*

The Joy Counter

People who are facing the end of their lives are some of the most joyful people I have ever known. Why? Maybe because they are living in the present moment and soaking it all in, rather than reliving the past or worrying about the future. Many have come to a place of acceptance and have addressed regrets from their past. They are letting go of stress, expectations, people-pleasing, and self-criticism. Their lifelong to-do list is dwindling to a few small tasks, mostly centered on matters of the heart.

Life gets complicated when we are working hard to prove our worth and find our way in this world, but as people slow down, expectations begin to fade away. They don't care so much about politics, the Grammy Awards, or the hottest new Netflix series. They don't need to fix, clean, or buy anything at all. Life gets simple when it slows down.

What's most meaningful becomes crystal clear. Holding hands, looking into the eyes of a grandchild, or laughing with friends is infinitely more important than being "productive" in any way. But most important, the walls often come down, allowing people to be authentic and real without fear of judgment. Hopefully, they are surrounded by love, which is the ultimate source of joy and comfort, especially when material items have become meaningless.

No one is better at seeing the joys our clients experience than hospice nurse and death doula Gabrielle Jimenez. Gabby has always looked for pockets of joy, whether as a little girl playing in nature or when sitting with someone who is dying.

She used to have a different nickname before we all called her Gabby. She used to be known as Cemetery Girl.

As a young girl, she received the unique moniker from the groundskeepers who often witnessed her slowly wandering alone through the cemetery. They noticed how she paused to read each headstone, one by one, until she finally picked out her spot. She would lay out a blanket, sit down, and snack on a sandwich or whatever she brought from home. When I heard this story, I knew we would become fast friends, as I also frequented our local cemetery when I was a little girl. Kindred spirits, I guess you could say.

Gabby had a rough childhood, filled with anger and verbal abuse. But, despite her challenging home life, she learned to see the world around her through rose-colored glasses and create a separate, more joyful world of her own where she was always able to find the good in everything. The cemetery offered Gabby a place to rest and be still. She found joy and wonder in the natural world and loved the outdoors, where all of this was free and available to her in great abundance.

Whether she was running along the riverbed laughing with friends, taking in the sweet smell of black licorice from the anise trees, or sitting quietly and contemplatively in the cemetery on her own, nature was a bright light in Gabby's otherwise troubled childhood. Whether it comes from nature or nurture, that seems to just be a fundamental part of who Gabby is. She always looks for joy, both in the big picture and in the details.

Over the years, Gabby has knocked on the doors of many dying people, and like she did as a little girl, she always looks for the good stuff. Those rose-colored glasses have served her well.

Gabby had one patient, Jacob, who was in his early forties and confined to a hospital bed because of an aggressive brain tumor called a glioblastoma. He had been a very active man, a cyclist who loved the outdoors and lived an adventurous life, but this "glio" robbed his body of the freedom to move.

Gabby compares the effects of a glio to watching a merry-go-round of changing sensory experiences. "With Jacob, he was always different when I saw him. Sometimes he could speak clearly, and sometimes he couldn't form sentences. Sometimes he could see clearly, and other times he was blind. His sensory responses were inconsistent, yet he was always kind, gentle, and happy to see me. He was pure joy."

Gabby and Jacob became so close over time that, on those days when he couldn't form a sentence, Gabby still knew what he was trying to say. These are the beautiful moments of our work, when we have the time to build a relationship and connect with someone's heart and soul.

When Gabby first stepped into Jacob's home, she couldn't help but notice the movie screen that covered the entire wall of his living room, in perfect view from Jacob's bed. Old movies, videos, and photos of his life played on the screen all day long. He watched them with great interest, laughing at certain moments, tearing up in others. As Gabby stood and watched, she couldn't help but smile at Jacob's gratitude and joy, despite his present situation.

When Gabby moved closer to sit by Jacob's bed, she noticed the unusually decorated grab bar that Jacob used to help pull himself up into a sitting position. Dangling from the bar were beaded bracelets, jeweled chakra chains, and a wide variety of other colorful mementos. Hanging in the middle of the bar was a little metal box, standing out among all the multicolored items.

"What's that?" asked Gabby.

"That's my joy counter," responded Jacob.

Gabby touched it and looked closer. "What's a joy counter?"

Jacob explained, "You know how when you go to a concert or ball game, they use a tally counter to keep track of everyone who enters? Well, I use this box to keep track of all the moments I feel joy each day." And then he added with a big smile, "So for me, it's a joy counter."

Jacob told Gabby that he had struggled with depression, watching his friends come and go, living their lives while he was stuck in a hospital bed. When he came up with the idea of the joy counter, it turned him around completely, and he began to see his life differently. He clicked the joy counter for visits from friends; for the unceasing and tender love from his wife, Carla; for the healthy foods she prepared; for pistachio ice cream, a good joke, and all the memories from his past that were being projected onto the wall.

"The more I used it, the more I realized how often I get to use it every day, Gabby. Once you begin to pay attention, you will discover that there is beauty and joy nearly everywhere."

"Wow, that's beautiful," Gabby responded. "I try to be positive, joyful, and pay attention to the good things in my life, but I've definitely never considered the benefits of counting my joy!" Gabby filed this idea away as a great one.

He looked at her with an inviting smile and said, "And sometimes... other people click it, too."

Gabby leaned forward toward the grab bar and pressed the joy counter.

"Why did you do that?" asked Jacob playfully.

"Because being here was my joy for the day."

"What does it feel like to be here?" Jacob asked with a curious tone.

Gabby shared from her heart. "Today you have reminded me how precious life is. You reminded me not to take life for granted and to notice the beauty all around me. You're right, Jacob, there's so much to be thankful for, and I'm going to start counting my joys, just like you."

For the next few months, Gabby visited Jacob weekly. They never shared the typical hello. Instead, every time she entered his home, she walked over to the grab bar, clicked the metal box, and said, "This is my joy for the day."

And every time Gabby was preparing to leave, Jacob would click the metal box and say, "This was my joy for the day."

On one visit, Gabby brought her two kittens, Ziggy and Zebulon, to meet Jacob. She laid them on his chest, and they purred, played, and cuddled. Jacob was delighted and couldn't stop clicking his joy counter. Gabby found a sweet spot that truly filled Jacob's heart. She left feeling like she had done something really good that day.

If she had a joy counter, she would have clicked it a hundred times.

A couple of weeks before Jacob died, Gabby came by for a visit. Carla was there, feeding him another home-cooked, healthy meal. Carla was always joyful, too, even though her world stopped as Jacob's world stopped . . . the caregiver and the dying person locked in a very long, slow dance.

Gabby pressed the joy counter, smiled, and sat next to Jacob as always.

Jacob looked over at Carla. "Do you think we should give Gabby her own joy counter?"

"I'm sitting right next to you. I can hear every word," Gabby said with a laugh. "And yes, yes! I'd love my own joy counter!"

Carla pulled out a box filled with joy counters and let Gabby pick which color she wanted. She picked a bright blue box that made her think of a favorite source of joy, the sky. From that day forward, Gabby began clicking her joy. She clicked the joy counter for the beautiful blue sky, as well as rainbows, clouds, sunsets, rain, and the special moments she noticed throughout the day.

The morning after Jacob died, Gabby woke up thinking about his life and looked over at the joy counter that sat next to her bedside. She reached over and clicked it, thinking about all that Jacob brought to her life.

She walked outside with her morning coffee and looked at the sky and the white, pillowy clouds, taking it all in. Jacob reminded her that life is fragile, and she didn't want to ever take the sky, or the clouds, or anything in her life for granted, so she clicked her joy counter again in deep reverence for our beautiful, natural world.

The clouds passed, and Gabby thought of life's miracles. "This is all free. We have been gifted so, so much. I don't want to miss another moment."

She went back inside her warm house, turned on some music, made breakfast, and then sat on her cozy couch and cuddled her cats.

A warm home. Music. Food. A cozy couch. Cats.

She reached into her pocket.

Click . . . click . . . click . . . click . . . click.

Joy in the everyday moments.

There was a knock on Gabby's front door. It was a delivery from Whole Foods.

Click.

She pulled one of her favorite treats out of the bag. Black licorice.

Click.

She sat on the couch and smelled the licorice before taking one little bite, instantly bringing back the most beautiful childhood memories.

She instinctively reached back in her pocket.

Click. Click. Click . . .

Count your joys. Count the beautiful moments. Even in the midst of the hard stuff, there is beauty everywhere.

Sometimes you just need to look for it.

LESSON #28

Don't forget to count your joys.

Final Thoughts

Dear Readers,

My hope is that within these pages you have had a chance to get to know some of the beautiful souls I have been so privileged to companion through the end of their lives, and the lessons they've left behind for all of us. I will likely continue to work with the dying until I find myself needing a death doula of my own one day. There is still so much I have left to learn. Even during the writing of this book, new clients have taught me new lessons.

"Define your habits or your habits will define you."

Mel, age 71

"Failure doesn't mean you failed. It means you tried."

Rico, age 58

"Don't seek perfection. Seek experiences."   *Kiki, age 39*

I've changed profoundly because of the work I do. I'm still undeniably and ridiculously human, but my clients have generously shared meaningful ways for me to change the way I live my life. If I were to sum it up in one short synopsis, I would tell you that the dying have taught me to live an inspired life.

Many people wonder what I think happens after we die. I have my own belief system to guide me in my daily life, and I hope you do, too, but the mystery of the afterlife is still just that . . . a mystery. Based on the time I've spent with people in that liminal space between this life and the great unknown, I believe with every fiber of my being that our ancestors will show up and carry us with loving arms into whatever it is that comes next.

Perhaps the mystery of the afterlife is similar to the mystery of birth. Have you ever wondered what babies might be thinking right before they are born? There they are in the womb, fully functioning, calm, cozy, and clueless that they are about to grow at least three times longer than they are, gain over a hundred pounds, and start walking around the outside of a planet. I don't think they would have ever guessed in a million years what they were getting into here, and that's how I feel about the afterlife. I'm curious and excited to discover what happens after this . . . and I will someday, when my time comes. Until then, I will gladly wait here with you.

While I'm waiting, I will continue to be inspired by those who are just one year old, those who are one hundred years old, and everyone in between. Their stories, their courage, and the goodness that exists in our hurting world gives me hope. We can do this, as long as we pay attention to what matters most. The lessons are tucked away in the pages of this book. We need each other. We always have. We always will. Be kind. Show up and finish well. Slow down. Choose love. Have faith. Share your heart. Let go. Count your joys. These are the things that carry us through.

Some of these might come easier to you than others. It took me decades to learn to love myself. I still struggle, and my greatest wish for you would be to learn to love yourself now . . . today . . . right this minute. It's so difficult to lean into the other lessons if we are busy being cruel to ourselves. You're beautiful. Look in the mirror and let yourself shine. See your beauty. Don't wait for a terminal diagnosis. Do it now.

And while you're at it . . . light the candles; let your hair blow in the wind; make a big, bright batch of your very own pink glitter; and sprinkle it everywhere.

ACKNOWLEDGMENTS

This book exists because Maria Shriver saw something in my work that I had not seen myself. Thank you, Maria, for reaching out with an idea that inspired me to dig even deeper into the countless lessons and blessings that have come from this sacred work. Your curiosity and desire to live with meaning and truth are an inspiration.

A special thanks to author and editor Meghan Rabbitt, who was willing to take a chance on a new writer for a column in Maria Shriver's *Sunday Paper*, the genesis for this book. Your support and camaraderie as we navigate this terrain together have meant the world to me.

Thank you to my agent, Bonnie Solow, from Solow Literary Enterprises, for first embracing this project, then for gently tending to all the twists and turns, and most of all for making this a smooth and joyful experience.

To my editor from Penguin Random House, Isabelle Alexander, you give me hope for future generations. Your professionalism and talent are undeniable, but your willingness to explore topics of death, dying, and meaning in life with such enthusiasm is so refreshing and appreciated. Your vision and perspective added so much to this book.

Thank you to the exceptionally outstanding team at Penguin Random House who have all added their personal touches to bring this book to life. Your wisdom, creativity, and experience kept me calm and gave me that gift of knowing that everything was just as it was meant to be. With appreciation to Meg Leder, editorial director; Brian Tart, president and publisher; Kate Stark, senior vice president and associate publisher; and everyone at Shriver Media. I would like to thank the production team, including Nick Michal, managing editor; Mike Brown, production editor; Tess Espinoza, director of production editorial; Nina Brown, production manager; Angelina Krahn, copyeditor; and proofreaders Nicole Celli and Kate Griggs. Thank you to everyone who contributed to the design of the book, including Jason Ramirez, art director; Lynn Buckley, cover designer; and Alexis Sulaimani, interior designer. Finally, thank you to our publicity and marketing staff, Julia Faulkner and Raven Ross; Mary Stone, director of marketing; Rebecca Marsh, director of publicity; and Shelby Meizlik, executive publicist.

A heartfelt thank-you to my husband, Mark Button, and our daughter, Hannah Button, who each dedicated precious days to reading my manuscript in its various stages, offering meaningful feedback, and encouraging me to share these stories with an open and full heart.

Creating this book would have been impossible without the sincere privilege of companioning my clients and their loved ones, who graciously shared their lives, their stories, and their final thoughts and moments with me. To all who have chosen me to be part of their end-of-life journey, you will always have a special place in my doula heart. An extra special thank-you to Pete and Carol Arnold, Marilyn

Brandwein, Penelope Butterfield, Janet Friedman, Karen Herzog, Dan Holzner, George and Grace Lee, Maria Sanders, Greg Wagner, and Priscilla Yue.

For me, doula work is best with a team. I'm a better doula because of my Bay Area End of Life Doula Alliance partners, our local doctors, hospice nurses, and social workers, and my colleagues who are featured in this book, including Franck Battelli, Dr. Joshua Biddle, Greg Brown, Dr. Virginia Chang, Lori Goldwyn, Sarah Hill, Gabrielle "Gabby" Jimenez LVN CHPLN, Redwing Keyssar RN, Chaplain Clarence Liu, and Angela Shook.

Thank you to my colleagues at the University of Vermont, including my fellow instructors and our program team, who work together to teach and support doulas and compassionate companions around the world. A very special shout-out to Colleen Fabian. You model the doula voice, the doula heart, and the doula way of being. Your gentle, peaceful presence is an inspiration to us all.

Deep gratitude to end-of-life caregivers and doulas everywhere who are compassionately dedicated to bringing emotional, practical, and unbiased support for those nearing death. I'm grateful for those who have helped guide my doula practice, including NEDA, AADM, INELDA, BTBH, Going with Grace, and all the other individuals and organizations who have come together to support and elevate this important work.

Deep gratitude to end-of-life caregivers and doulas everywhere who are compassionately dedicated to bringing emotional, practical, and unbiased support for those nearing death.

To my very patient and hilarious family, thank you for providing the levity and the caffeine. Nights spent talking about death and brainstorming inappropriate book titles are forever imprinted in my memory. This work can be heavy, and it's always important to also see the joy. Thank you for constantly reminding me of that.

Mark, you are my partner in every way. It would take another full book to explain all the goodness and love you have added to my life.

Carly, you are a survivor and a seeker. I'm inspired to watch the fire igniting under your feet as you rise up and make a positive difference in so many lives.

Jack, you are simply a wonderful human being with impeccable integrity and compassion for all. I'm honored to be your mom.

Hannah, your intelligence and your quick wit have kept me afloat this past year. Spending time together and working with you is pure joy.

And finally, thank you to my mom, Rosemary Steiss; my brother, Tony Renn; Joseph Sexson; Jasmin Voelz; loving and supportive friends close by and in faraway places; colleagues; fellow doulas and death workers; people on airplanes and in bookstores; neighbors on dog walks; strangers in grocery lines; and anyone else who has taken the time to be curious about this topic and share their hearts and stories with me along the way.

I am forever grateful.

Diane

There are many wonderfully creative and thought-provoking tools that doulas use to support our clients to live fully as they prepare for their end-of-life journeys. The good news is that you can take advantage of many of these tools right now. They are life-changing for anyone, at any age!

This section is an invitation for you to explore who and what are most important in your life and to identify ways to shift toward a life filled with more meaning, joy, peace, and contentment. These exercises are designed for you to reflect on the stories and the lessons in this book and to then discover how to incorporate these insights into your everyday life.

With curiosity, an open heart, and a willingness to explore, you can live a life filled with what matters most . . . to you.

Self-Love

One of the greatest lessons the dying teach us is that it is impossible to fully love others if we don't first learn to love ourselves. In "Damn, You're Beautiful," you learned about my personal journey with self-love through the story of my cancer diagnosis. After a life-long struggle, I finally saw my beauty. This exercise is an invitation to see the beauty in yourself, just as I learned to see it that day I stared at myself in the mirror. If you can learn to treat yourself as you would treat your best friend, you might let go of the harsh judgments and criticisms that you carry. Although it might not come naturally to you, pausing to be kind to yourself fosters a free spirit and an untethered heart. If I can do it, you can, too.

This exercise has two parts, and both are about self-love.

Part one: Before you begin your day, take a minute to look at yourself in the mirror. This is meant to be not just a quick glance but a deep gaze into your own eyes. Really look deeply at yourself and remember that you were once a small child. Smile, see your beauty, be gentle, and give yourself a blessing to open up and receive whatever goodness comes your way today. You deserve it.

Part two: Prepare for the next step by recording your voice reciting the meditation below, if possible. If not, you can read it out loud, but it is much more powerful if you record it so you can be still for just one minute and listen to the power of your own voice reminding you that you are loving and lovable. Slow down, feel the words, and give yourself permission to believe them.

Pure Love—A Meditation

I am pure love.
I offer kindness to all beings.
I am beautiful on the inside.

I am in awe of the miracle that is my body.

I am confident and fully alive.

I practice compassion and loving-kindness for all living things.

I practice humility, grace, and forgiveness.

I am consciously building my legacy each and every day.

I am discovering beauty all around me.

I find joy in the simplicity of an ordinary day.

I pay attention to my passions.

I am living a life of purpose.

I am generous.

I share my heart, my time, and my gifts with others.

I am kind to myself.

I pause to reflect before I respond.

I remember to say "thank you."

I remember to say "I'm sorry."

I remember to say "I love you."

I am here to give and receive love.

I am making a difference.

I know my life matters.

The world is a better place because I am here.

I belong here.

I am at peace.

I am pure love.

Try both of these exercises every morning for a week and see how it feels. Over time, you will hopefully learn to be more gentle and kind to yourself.

A Mini Life Review

Doulas often start connecting and building relationships by talking about topics that are joyful for most people, like food, music, and love. These universal topics can spark memories and encourage conversation. This often reveals what is most meaningful for that particular person. Take for example Miss Sally, whose love of music and adventure brought her a lifetime of meaningful moments, and also laid the foundation for conversations about what mattered most to her in the end.

We know that no one is holding on to hundred-dollar bills or fancy car keys when they die. They are holding the hands of family, friends, and those who have cared for them. They are holding on to stories and memories tucked into their hearts. They are holding hopes for goodness, peace, and joy in the lives of those they are leaving behind. In the end, it's all about love.

For this exercise you will need some paper, a pen, and a quiet space to contemplate. Think back to the introduction of this book and the story about the final meal my grandfather shared with his family, where he listened to his favorite music and spoke about how much he was going to miss his favorite condiment, mint jelly. What would your version of that be?

Begin by imagining that you are gathered for a dinner with those you love. Imagine the faces of those you have invited to join you for one of your final gatherings. Notice how it feels to be surrounded by the people you love the most.

Who is there? Write their names. Choose from your own heart, without any sense of obligation. These are your special people.

Imagine the ambiance. Imagine your table, warmly decorated to your liking. Are you outdoors or gathered around a favorite dining table? Is there soft lighting, string lights, or candles?

What is the environment like? Describe the little details that would let you know that this table was set just for you.

And what about the music? Are you playing music from your past or current favorites? Music helps tell the story of our lives.

What music will be playing? Create a short playlist of the songs you might want to hear if it were your final occasion with loved ones.

Food brings us together and nurtures us physically, emotionally, and spiritually. It connects us to our culture and traditions, and ties us to the people around us. Imagine you are planning a final meal for yourself and all your guests who have joined you.

What's for dinner? Describe the meal and why you chose it.

.

This time together is an opportunity to share your heart with your closest people. Imagine this might be the last time you see them, and the last time you will all be together in one space. Take a moment to look at each person, one by one.

What will you miss most? Write about what you will miss about those you love and what you will miss about your one big, beautiful life. Share the words percolating in your heart.

.

We know that, at the end of life, we want to feel that our life has had meaning and that we will not be forgotten.

What do you want people to remember about you? Write it down. Some clients have shared that this question brings up reminders of people they haven't apologized to, or people they may want to thank for the impact they have had on their lives. Contemplate this, too.

.

After contemplating these questions, you might want to reflect even further with a more detailed life review. When you consider the passing decades of your life, how have you changed? How would you describe yourself now? What are your most poignant memories? What have you learned about life that you would want to share with future generations? There is so much to explore within our own hearts!

This simple exercise offers an opportunity to pause and reflect on your past, while also gently considering the future and what might matter most in the end.

Everyday Gratitude

In the chapter "Don't Waste Your Gratitude," we learned that even unspoken words of gratitude can be a form of unfinished business. Sometimes it is not the big regrets that keep the dying up at night, but the fact that they never thanked their sixth-grade teacher for the extra tutoring, or the deli worker who always let them sample the cheese before buying it.

Sometimes we rush through our days without paying attention to all the people who support us along the way. I think of the farmers, the truckers, and the grocery store workers who all came together to get this one head of lettuce into the produce section for me to take home for my nightly salad. These days most of us are served by so many others—postal workers, nurses, the garbage pickup crew, bank tellers, flight attendants, auto mechanics, restaurant workers, and all those people who repair our roads, maintain our parks, and serve us in ways we may not ever even think about.

Gratitude exercises are powerful. They cause us to look at the bright side of life and to appreciate what we do have rather than dwelling on what we don't. Journaling and daily gratitude practices keep us connected to those we know and love. But what about those we have never met? These prompts encourage you to expand your circle of gratitude. You might consider trying some of these exercises in addition to any ways you are currently expressing your heart.

1. Get to know your local grocery clerk, barista, or someone you see on a regular basis but rarely truly connect with. Greet them by name the next time you see them.

2. Say "thank you" to someone you speak to during your day today. Take the time to be specific. "Thank you for bagging my groceries." Or "I really appreciate how much time you have taken to explain this to me."

3. Engage in a conversation with a stranger. Remember, your simple words might be the highlight of their day.

4. Reach out to someone you care about but haven't talked to in a while. Tell them what they mean to you and how they have affected your life.

Everyday Joy

Remember "The Joy Counter" and the positivity and gratitude that came along with noticing the simple pleasures of an ordinary day? What about in your life? What are the simple routines and the beautiful moments that you experience each day? This exercise helps you tune in to your joy, and even helps you look for joy where you may not normally notice it.

If you think you might want to pay attention to your joy on a regular basis, you may want to purchase a "joy counter," or a hand tally, but for this exercise you can use your phone or a piece of paper to pay attention to your joy for just one day.

Every time you feel joy, see something beautiful, or feel grateful, click your hand tally, or write it down. Pay attention to the unexpected sources of joy . . .

Your dog puts his head on your lap.

Your neighbor waves from across the street.

You notice a heart-shaped rock on your morning walk.

A hummingbird feeds on the flowers outside your window.

The sun shines on your face.

The familiar taste of your morning coffee, just how you like it.

You open your mailbox and see a handwritten letter from a friend.

A favorite song from years ago comes on the radio.

A driver lets you move into their lane.

Your hair is blowing in the breeze.

Warm water comes out of your shower.

You climb into bed with clean sheets.

At the end of the day, take a look back at all the beautiful moments from your day. Try it for a week if you enjoyed it. Soon you will learn to see the everyday moments of your life in a new and inspiring way!

So Much More Than Fine

People who are dying and have called a death doula are wanting to talk about what they are experiencing. They rarely tell me they are just "fine." They tell me they are feeling weak, frightened, peaceful, frustrated, curious, introspective, exhausted, bored, anxious, accepting, worried, loved, overwhelmed, sad, calm, or whatever might be coming up for them that day. Sometimes they are experiencing several of these emotions all at once. The everyday, convenient words aren't expressive or deep enough. They are feeling so much more than that. As complex human beings, we are all so much more than just "fine."

In the story "You Are Not Fine," you learned about the impact of sincerely opening up to people about how you are doing, and how liberating it can be to allow yourself to be more than just "fine." You also learned how empowering it can be to be honest about how you are feeling, even if it isn't always positive.

Try to spend an entire week answering the question "How are you?" with honesty, accuracy, and truth. When someone asks you how you are feeling, take it as an opportunity to pause and practice a moment of self-reflection about how you really are doing at that moment.

Avoid saying:

"I'm fine."

"I'm OK."

"I'm good."

"I'm so busy."

Another way of doing this exercise is to contemplate this question throughout your day, starting with when you first wake up each morning. Then set an alarm to go off three or four times during the day. Each time you hear the alarm, pause and ask yourself how you are feeling at that time. Then ask yourself again before going to bed at night.

Keep a list of the words you use to express how you are feeling that week, and you will see your emotions more clearly. And if you find yourself feeling "busy," ask yourself what you are busy doing. Is it something you enjoy? Or something you don't? Sometimes these answers, and the patterns of our emotions, can lead to significant and healthy life changes.

Fill Your Cups

Think back to the story of my daughter Carly leading our family through an intention-setting activity for New Year's Eve using the idea of our many "cups of life." Every day we make decisions about how we invest our time and energy, but how often do we stop to consider how all aspects of our lives are coming together for our greatest good? This exercise is designed to help you live a more balanced life by considering all your cups.

For this exercise, imagine your life as a series of eight cups, and your time and energy as the water filling them. If you have a set of eight bowls or drinking glasses, you can use them with a pitcher of water to complete this exercise. Some clients like to use colored water to see clearly. Label the "cups" and fill each of them to the level you feel is an appropriate representation of how you are doing today.

You may notice that some of your cups are full and getting lots of attention, while some have been neglected far too long.

Contemplate and imagine . . .

Your social cup

Your health and fitness cup

Your spirituality cup

Your relationships cup

Your career cup

Your financial security cup

Your self-care and emotional wellness cup

Your peace and calm cup

Which of your cups are full? Which of your cups are empty . . . or low? Which cups are overflowing or maybe getting too much of your precious time and energy? Which cups have you not paid attention to for a long time?

One cup at a time, pause to honor where you are. Meet yourself with love and acceptance. Make a plan to dig into the areas that need some special tending this coming year.

You deserve to live a balanced life with full and meaningful cups.

The Final Checklist

Throughout this book, you have heard stories from the dying. While many are heart-wrenching, most of them ended with our clients feeling a deep sense of peace, comfort, and love. Those who had time were given an opportunity to heal broken relationships, let go of guilt and shame, address issues of forgiveness, open their hearts, share their stories, create legacy projects, and prepare to die well.

We have learned that the most direct path to dying well is to live well. In "The Final Checklist," we were reminded to contemplate life's most important questions now. Sadly, some people wait too long. This exercise can guide you to that place of deep internal peace, starting today.

Personally, I do this exercise once a month and encourage you to do it, too. I contemplate each question carefully. If there is someone I need to say "thank you," "I'm sorry," or "I love you" to, I pick up the phone or write a note and make sure it gets done. I pay attention to my worries. Identifying them is the first step to working through them. Sometimes they require professional counseling or a hard conversation, and that's OK. I pay attention to what matters and focus on allowing time and energy to experience as much joy as possible in my life.

For this exercise, answer the Final Checklist questions yourself. You can do this once, or on a regular basis. I've found that a monthly review allows me to stay current, keep a clean slate, and avoid collecting unfinished business as the years go by.

1. Who matters most?

2. What matters most?

3. What worries you when lying awake in bed at night?

4. What brings you joy when you are awake in the daytime?

5. What is left unsaid?

6. What is left undone?

Once you've gone through these questions and tended to what came up for you, you may discover that some issues are still left lingering. We cannot control what happens to us, but we can control how we respond. For the things that you cannot change, these two questions can help you to face them with more ease and identify ways to be gentle with yourself in the process.

1. What brings you comfort?

2. What brings you peace?

Knowing what brings you comfort and peace can guide you toward joy and stillness and can offer a calm way of being in our fast-paced, hectic world. If you keep a journal of these entries, you will see the ebbs and flows of your life, and the changes and growth that happen through the years. We are always changing. Let's always change for the better.

May we all love more deeply,
share our hearts more freely,
and remember that every day is a chance
to say "I love you" just one more time.